Milton's Language

THE LANGUAGE LIBRARY

EDITED BY DAVID CRYSTAL

Milton's Language

THOMAS N. CORNS

Basil Blackwell

PR
3596
C67
1990

Copyright © Thomas N. Corns 1990

First published 1990

Basil Blackwell Ltd
108 Cowley Road, Oxford, OX4 1JF, UK

Basil Blackwell, Inc.
3 Cambridge Center
Cambridge, Massachusetts 02142, USA

British Library Cataloguing in Publication Data

A CIP catalogue record for this book is available from the British Library.

Library of Congress Cataloging in Publication Data

Corns, Thomas N.
    Milton's language / Thomas N. Corns.
        p.   cm.   — (The Language Library)
    Includes bibliographical references.
    ISBN 0–631–15145–1
    1. Milton, John, 1608–1674—Language—Grammar. 2. English
language—Early modern, 1500–1700—Grammar. I. Title. II. Series.
PR3596.C67   1990
821'.4—dc20
                                                        89–38705
                                                            CIP

Typeset in 11 on 13 pt Times Roman
by Vera-Reyes Inc., Philippines
Printed in Great Britain by T. J. Press Ltd, Padstow, Cornwall

For Pat, in lieu of many ornaments

Contents

List of Tables and Figures

Acknowledgements

Colleagues and fellow-Miltonists have been very generous with information, suggestions, useful argument, offprints and access to their work in progress. David Lindsay reminded me of the Blakean Milton at critical moments and offered useful eighteenth-century analogues to Miltonic practice. Ian Gregson advised on prosody and lineation. John Leonard showed me chapters from his forthcoming *Naming in Paradise: Milton and the Language of Adam and Eve*, which gave me a richer sense of the role of punning in the war in Heaven. Archie Burnett, too, generously showed me unpublished work on lineation. H. Neville Davies confirmed a notion about 'Lycidas'. Both David Crystal and Gordon Campbell read the typescript. John Borland advised me on sampling procedures and the design of the more statistical aspects of the study of lexis. Steve Jones wrote for me programs to extract a random sample of line numbers and to run more conveniently the Oxford Concordance Program. The Text Archive of Oxford University Computing Service supplied me with a computer-readable version of *Paradise Lost*, and Noel Heather supplied *Paradise Regained*. Sue Bond typed the minor poetry on to disk. I am grateful to Longman for their permission to produce computer-readable transcriptions of the edition of John Carey and Alastair Fowler and for permission to quote from that edition, and to Methuen for permission to quote from *Jacobean and Caroline Poetry*, edited by T. G. S. Cain. The Computing Laboratory and the Library of the University College of North Wales were unfailingly helpful.

Abbreviations and Editions Used

Poems
: *The Poems of John Milton*, edited by John Carey and Alastair Fowler (London: Longman, 1980; first published 1968). All references to Milton's poems are to the 1980 edition unless otherwise stated.

CPW
: *Complete Prose Works of John Milton*, edited by Don M. Wolfe et al. (New Haven: Yale University Press, 1953–82). All references to Milton's prose are to this edition.

Campbell
: *John Milton: The Complete Poems*, edited by Gordon Campbell, text edited by B. A. Wright (London and New York: Dent and Dutton, 1980).

OED
: *The Oxford English Dictionary*.

Var. Comm.
: *A Variorum Commentary on the Poems of John Milton*, edited by Douglas Bush et al. (London: Routledge and Kegan Paul, 1970–).

1

Milton Studies: Past, Present and in Prospect

From the first edition of William Empson's *Milton's God* (1961) to the publication late in 1968 of the Longman annotated edition of his poems, the 1960s constituted a decade of glittering achievement in Milton studies.[1] My debt to the scholarship and criticism of that era is both pervasive and obvious. Four mutually very dissimilar works of the period made contributions of special importance to the appreciation of the style of Milton's vernacular poetry: *Milton's Grand Style* by Christopher Ricks, *Milton's Grammar* by Ronald David Emma, *Surprised by Sin* by Stanley Eugene Fish and the Longman edition itself.[2]

Ricks's account is to some extent locked into the more unprofitable exchanges of the 1930s and after. Dr Johnson's famous animosity to Milton's language, the charge, inherited from earlier eighteenth-century Miltonists, that it is in some respects unEnglish,[3] was revived in the influential interpretations of T. S. Eliot and F. R. Leavis, whose devaluation probably has more to do with ideological history than with close response to style.[4] Leavis had concluded that 'Milton has forgotten the English language', that his style 'barred Milton from essential expressive resources of English', that 'a good deal of *Paradise Lost* strikes one as being almost as mechanical as bricklaying'.[5] For Eliot, even in his more sympathetic response to the verse,

there is always the maximal, never the minimal, alteration of ordinary language. Every distortion of construction, the foreign idiom, the use of a word in a foreign way or with the meaning of the foreign word from which it is derived rather than the accepted meaning in English, every idiosyncrasy is a particular act of violence which Milton has been the first to commit. There is no cliché, no poetic diction in the derogatory sense, but a perpetual sequence of original acts of lawlessness.[6]

Earlier he had charged him with doing 'damage to the English language' of an abiding kind.[7] In both his essays, the case against Milton rests largely on his supposed unEnglishness. A large emptiness seemingly characterizes the oeuvre.

Ricks sets himself a polemical task, as his fighting title suggests: 'grandness' in poetry is of dubious value to the Leavisites. His case against Leavis and those who adopted his perspective rests on the demonstration that passages of *Paradise Lost* prove tractable to close readings demonstrative of the complexity, the ambiguity, the subtlety of Milton's lexis, syntax and imagery. His verse appears in Ricks's readings as precise, expressive and demanding, and thus it meets those aesthetic criteria which Leavis perceives to be satisfied in the Elizabethan and Jacobean poets whom he admired. Developing an approach which Empson had entertained decades earlier,[8] Ricks draws on the insights of early editors, of Richard Bentley, Patrick Hume, the Richardsons and Thomas Newton, whose commentaries isolate with admirable precision what seem to them points of deviance, obscurity and felicity in the text. But mostly Ricks's case rests on the elegant ingenuity of his own critical acumen. His book examines closely about 100 passages from *Paradise Lost* – sometimes no longer than a single line – less than 500 lines in all. Questions about the typicality of his examples or the distinctiveness of the features he identifies are not consistently addressed, and Milton's achievements appear curiously decontextualized from the practices of earlier and contemporary poets. Nevertheless, *Milton's Grand Style* offers a range of local insights of abiding value and a generally persuasive revaluation of Milton's art.

Emma complements Ricks's achievement – more methodical, deeply concerned with isolating what is distinctively 'Miltonic', and concerned, too, with directing what Ricks had termed 'The Milton Controversy' towards a calmer scientificism where differences could be defined and resolved. Interpretively, his study fails badly. Despite prefatory denials, much of *Milton's Grammar* offers mere lists of statistics, of the occurrence of so many prepositions or pronouns in this or that form, with little consideration of how such information illuminates our response to the text. Furthermore, the design of his study fails to satisfy the rigorous expectations his methodology raises. His analysis is based on just over 8,000 words drawn roughly equally from Milton's poetry and prose. While such a sample may allow Emma to draw significant conclusions about pervasive phenomena such as accidence, it will not serve for larger features, such as sentence structure (he has fewer than 140 sentences of Milton's poetry in his sample), nor will it trap important lexical features distributed unevenly through the texts. Moreover, Shakespeare and T. S. Eliot, the authors he uses for comparison with Milton, are generically and chronologically remote from him: difference could merely reflect the different norms of dissimilar genres and other periods. The samples from the 'controls' are utterly inadequate. Yet Emma's contribution is not negligible. On some small-scale features, such as Milton's general avoidance of the rather antique '-th' inflection of third-person singular verbs, his findings should probably stand, and some of his objectives remain both worthwhile and realizable, though Fowler's remark that 'this work of Emma's may be the first of a series of more objective and descriptive studies of Milton's style' (*Poems*, p. 430) rings poignantly twenty years on.

Fish's inclusion here may surprise: as we shall see, he appears in a fiercely adversarial posture against stylistics. Yet *Surprised by Sin* has some notable comments on the minutiae of Miltonic writing. It embraces different issues from those that exercised Ricks and Emma – A. J. A. Waldock's *Paradise Lost and its Critics*,[9] not *Revaluation*, determines the critical battleground. Yet Fish's study, an early and important stage in the development of that American version of reader-response criticism in which he figures centrally, offers, in effect, a series of close readings which are not remote from the Ricksian methodology. His critical focus is on the processes by which the readers' perceptions form, cohere, wander, resolve and re-form. He and Emma would disagree *toto caelo* about the modality in which Milton's text exists. For the latter it shares the same objective reality as bank accounts and coffee spoons. It may be measured, counted, summed up in terms of categories which define formal characteristics thought to inhere within it. For Fish, the text abides in the perceptions of its readers. As we shall see, negotiating that conflict is central to the development of a revived stylistics.

The edition of Carey and Fowler builds confidently on the work of others. Fowler's view of *Paradise Lost* owes much to Ricks's conception of the wit, flexibility and subtlety of Milton's texture. He draws, too, in a guarded way on the work of Emma and on an early, limited but nevertheless very useful account by Lalia Phipps Boone of the language of *Paradise Lost* Book VI.[10] Fowler's disagreement often seems as much with the received tradition of eighteenth-century scholarship as with the Leavisite position. Persistently, he asserts against claims that Milton is using words in ways reminiscent of Latin usage, the Englishness of his practices. Carey's annotation of the minor poems, and particularly of those written before 1645, points to his pervasive debts to an earlier tradition of English poetry, to Spenser, to Shakespeare, to Sylvester. His place as heir to Elizabethan traditions – and linguistic practice – emerges powerfully. Fowler's introduction to *Paradise Lost* and Carey's headnotes, particularly to *Comus* and *Samson Agonistes*, offer stylistic comment of a terse astuteness, and the edition as a whole presents, in a distributed form, perhaps the best single account of Milton's style.

Towards the end of the 1960s and into the early 1970s adjacent disciplines seemed to function as important catalysts to stylistic studies. Richard Ohmann in North America and J. P. Thorne in the United Kingdom elegantly demonstrated the adaptability of the concepts and categories of Chomskyan linguistics to the analysis of literary texts, while Roger Fowler, in a series of publications, adapted a more eclectic linguistics to good purpose.[11] 'Linguistic stylistics', which in English studies had existed in embryo since the late 1950s,[12] had come to full term. Simultaneously, early computer-based studies – pre-eminently Milic's account of Swift's prose style – presented possibilities for processing literary data on a new scale and with a new precision.[13]

Yet only a little has been achieved. A. C. Partridge, in *The Language of Renaissance Poetry*, effectively demonstrated important continuities in lexical practice between Milton and the Spenserian tradition, though he accepts perhaps too readily some of Emma's findings, nor can so wide a study address the more intricate questions of syntax in much depth.[14] Again, J. B. Broadbent, especially in his primarily pedagogic *Paradise Lost: Introduction*, built intelligently on the conclusions of Fowler to indicate with some perception directions which a study of Milton's language could take.[15] Burnett's account of Milton's minor poetry effectively dismantled much received opinion about its style and developed a series of sensitive observations within a linguistic-stylistic methodology.[16] My own account of Milton's prose asserted its Englishness, defined what is distinctive about its lexis, syntax and imagery, and pointed to the way in which it develops. But most Milton criticism has addressed different questions and adopted different methodologies.[17]

Milton's politics and the interpretation of the ideological implications of his writings seem the principal foci of the present decade. Christopher Hill's political biography of Milton reinvigorated earlier debates, and the twin impulses of the New Historicism and Marxisms old and new have motivated some of the more important critical effort of the recent past. It is an approach I myself have found congenial and productive.[18] Lacanian, Derridian and feminist interpretation have become significant traditions in Milton studies, and where linguistic models are invoked, neither Firth nor Chomsky figures, but rather the semiotic theories of Saussure.[19] I may cite two good indices of the state of Milton studies, Margarita Stocker's useful 'introduction to the variety of criticism' of *Paradise Lost* and the methodological distribution of papers presented to the Third International Milton Symposium of 1988. The former offers sections on thematic, historical, feminist, reader-response, genre theory, psychoanalytical and mythic readings: style is treated briefly and in passing.[20] Of the more in ninety papers presented at the symposium, only a handful dealt even secondarily with questions about Milton's language.[21]

At the same time as that deconstructionist–feminist–historicist axis absorbs much of the more innovative energies in Milton studies, so too a major theoretical critique of the methodology further inhibits the revitalization of linguistic stylistics. Stanley Fish's belligerent but cogent essay, 'What Is Stylistics and Why Are They Saying Such Terrible Things About It?', still works influentially as a dismissal of the undertaking as practised by Milic, Ohmann and Thorne.[22] His argument focuses on the interpretative link between the identification of (or attribution to) the text of formal characteristics and the postulation of a semantic value for those characteristics. Referring specifically to Milic's work on Swift but implying a larger criticism of the whole undertaking, he observes that:

> the procedure is not circular but arbitrary. The data are scrutinized and an interpretation is *asserted* for them, asserted rather than proven because there is nothing in the machinery Milic cranks up to authorize the leap (from the data to a specification of their value) he makes. What does authorize it is an unexamined and highly suspect assumption that one can read directly from the description of a text (however derived) to the shape or quality of its author's mind, in this case from the sheer quantity of verbal items to the largeness of the intelligence that produce them.[23]

Of Thorne, he concludes:

> It is not my intention flatly to deny any relationship between structure and sense, but to argue that if there is one, it is not to be explained by attributing an independent meaning to the linguistic facts, which will, in any case, mean differently in different circumstances.[24]

The faults which Fish identifies are real enough: that interpretive leap from linguistic description to critical reading defies the explicit scientificity which practitioners of the methodology claim as their own. But such research, if it eschews the interpretative dimension, offers nothing to its readers. What profits it to compute the parameters of a style if we may attribute no larger significance to the findings?

My stylistic criticism addresses directly the experience of reading, focusing on the relationship between readers' expectations and their perceptions of the text. Both expectation and perception, however, are historically determined. The cultural assumptions of Milton's original readers are inevitably part of the ideological superstructure of the mid-seventeenth century. Their

notions of registeral norms, the decorum of genres as they under-
stood it, differ sharply from those of our own age. Their linguistic
perspectives – indeed, their versions of the language itself – are
not ours: we are divided from them by three centuries of obsol-
escence, redundancy, growth, innovation and semantic shift.
Moreover, literary language, which works so delicately and yet so
powerfully through the recognition of complex intertexts,
changes in more subtle ways than non-literary language. Milton's
shopping lists, were they extant, would probably pose for most
modern readers no more difficulty of interpretation than my own,
but our perception of his poems inevitably is shaped by a familiarity with intervenient literary production. One cannot forget his
imitators as one responds to the original. We cannot, save patho-
logically, unlearn what we have learnt, unread what we have
read. The shift in cultural, literary, and linguistic assumptions
stands between. When Adam and Eve discuss 'manuring' Eden
(*Paradise Lost*, IV.628), we may recognize that the older meaning, merely 'cultivation', is uppermost, yet the line, provoking
association with steaming dungheaps, sounds incongruous to a
modern reader. The experience of reading a long Miltonic sentence probably demands much more from us than it would have
done from the seventeenth-century cultural elite. Rhetorical taste
and expectations have altered completely. No doubt Fowler is
right to observe of the rhetorical patterning:

> This was once a chief glory of the poem, but it is so little to the modern
> taste that any attempt to cultivate a discriminating appreciation of it
> would now be uphill work . . . The identification of all the schemes and
> tropes would not only be pedantry but useless and ignorant pedantry; for
> at its best rhetoric depended on a response much more sophisticated than
> the elementary one of recognition.[25]

Yet the seventeenth-century readers' expectations, in a provi-
sional and partial way reflective of the values of our own age, may
tentatively be reconstructed through that process of linguistic-
stylistic enquiry which I take here as my primary methodology.
Through resources of historical lexicography and by other tech-
niques we may work towards the identification of the status of the
words Milton used in the linguistic framework of his own day. We

may determine the elements of eccentricity or conformity in his linguistic practice by comparison with the norms of closely contemporary and situationally analogous writing. Thus, with difficulty and in tentative vein, we may come to perceive his text as once it would have been perceived, while retaining a sense of our own distance from those original perceptions. Some of the original pleasure of the text – in its freshness, its technical brilliance, its brave innovation and its extreme felicity – may be seen again. Fish claims to have redefined the activity of criticism 'so that it was no longer a matter of demonstration but a matter (endlessly negotiated) of persuasion'.[26] I think I accept that now. My object is to persuade modern readers to stand before the glories of the Miltonic oeuvre, much as they may stand before Botticelli's recently restored paintings, and to look upon them, if not as the original audience would have looked, then at least seeing them freed from the grimy accretions of the centuries.

This book falls into three major sections, and each addresses a separate aspect of Milton's style within a different investigative framework. Chapter 2, on sentence structure, reports a search to isolate and define those syntactic preferences which give to Milton's poetry a distinctiveness which many readers have felt but which, in my view, has escaped a proper exploration. Milton's practice is examined in close comparison with the norms of situationally similar writing. It has been necessary, while working on Milton, simultaneously to investigate the practices of contemporaries in order to establish these norms. In Baconian fashion, the structure of the exposition largely mirrors the process of the investigation. Necessarily, the account rests on rigorous statistical procedure and interpretation. It would have been inconceivable without recourse to a computer.

Chapter 3 is more implicity comparative. It sets Milton's vocabulary and the way he uses it against the achievements of contemporary poets and also earlier poets whose status and influence were recognized contemporaneously, and it attempts to relate Milton's poetry to wider aspects of English in the midseventeenth century. For a variety of reasons, it seemed improbable that norms could be constructed by the sort of sampling and analysis used in the previous chapter, so assessments of what was customary usage rest largely on historical lexicography, pre-eminently the evidence of the *Oxford English Dictionary*, supplemented by the occasional use of concordances. The availability of the *OED* on CD-ROM, which had extended to some seats of higher education (though not my own) as I researched this section, certainly permits statements about the extent of Miltonic neologisms and his extension to the semantic range of words to be made much less arduously and much more confidently. Yet that constitutes quite a limited advance in placing our response to Milton's language on a proper historical basis. Current computer technology could make available for interrogation and analysis large corpora of early modern texts, which in turn could disclose with a new precision and sensitivity the status of the lexis both of Milton and of his contemporaries. An appropriate level of funding and a considerable degree of co-operation and co-ordination are the sole requirements and 'the effects of such a Work would be wonderfully advantageous', as Bishop Sprat remarked in an earlier age of scientific opportunity.[27] Until that advance is effected, statistics about many aspects of lexis at best indicate merely the approximate scale of phenomena, and often function more as an aspect of rhetoric than of scientific exposition. Meanwhile, the best method for considering most aspects of lexical achievement is the accumulation of close readings of pertinent examples.

The assembly of information about word frequencies is a function which computers perform in abundance. Quite early concordance programs offered the facility for exhaustive statistical accounts of, within samples of text, how many words occur once, twice, thrice, etc. Moreover, the data, requiring no subjective categorization by the investigator, has a 'hardness' that especially recommends it to statistical analysis. Yet, paradoxically, the easier the figures are to assemble, the harder they are to interpret intelligently. For purposes of author identification or canonical investigation, information about the relative incidence of words in this or that text may be crucial. How such information may support a critical argument presents graver problems. Chapter 4, on word frequencies, offers a more tentative analysis.

2

Sentence Structure

The Structure of the Investigation

My larger purposes, in this as in other parts of the study, are not only to account for the characteristics of Milton's style in terms which accord with twentieth-century linguistic classification, but also to define those ways in which his work may well have appeared to a contemporary reader approaching the oeuvre with literary expectations derived from an appreciation of the mid-seventeenth-century poetic tradition. To this end, much of my effort has been invested in the efficient reconstruction of the linguistic norms of contemporary and situationally analogous writing. What is characteristically Miltonic is to be perceived through its distinction from the stylistic practices of an appropriately constructed control.

I selected as my primary control the more closely contemporary sections of *Jacobean and Caroline Poetry: An Anthology*, edited by T. G. S. Cain (London and New York: Methuen, 1981), a well-edited and intelligently designed collection, which usefully includes, besides a preponderance of major writers (Herrick, Herbert, Carew, Crashaw, Marvell and Vaughan), a good range of other contemporaries, and thus produces what seems to me a likely cross-section of the material familiar to a poetry reader of the period.[1] However, the Milton canon has within it a far larger proportion of narrative poetry and poetry containing dialogue and set speeches than is to be found within the Cain anthology, and so I supplemented what may be termed the control group with material from a narrative poem from the 1640s, Abraham Cowley's *The Civil War*, and from another of the 1650s, Sir Richard Fanshawe's translation of *The Lusiads*; as representative of the 1660s, I took material from John Dryden's *Annus Mirabilis*.[2]

My account of sentence structure is based on the analysis of a large sample drawn from the Milton texts and those of the control group. Using a specially written computer program, I constructed a random sample of approximately one-in-ten of the lines of all the material, a total of approximately two and a half thousand sampling-points.[3] Each line was then examined, and, if a sentence began within it, I collected data relating to thirty variables appertaining to questions of syntax and prosody and their relationship. The information was gathered and encoded using a questionnaire designed for the purpose, and stored, manipulated and processed using SPSS[x], a versatile and well-documented suite of programs designed for statistical analysis and interpretation.[4] A total of 780 sentences were considered in this way, and my database for this section of the study contains more than 23,000 individual observations.

Punctuation and Sentence Structure

Analysis of sentence structure is scarcely feasible without some working definition of what a sentence is, and the at times rather scholastic wranglings of theoretical linguistics can seem unhelpful to the practical critic faced with making hundreds, perhaps thousands, of decisions in classification. Simple criteria are needed to determine where one sentence ends and the next begins.

In modern prose and in much of modern poetry, the readiest guide is punctuation. Of course, there are texts both in modernist creative writing and in such aberrant and traditional registers as legal documentation, for example, where punctuation's normal implications are suspended, but generally speaking, in accurate English, sentences begin with capital letters and end with full-stops, question marks or exclamation marks. In early modern English, however, matters are more complicated.

The seventeenth century was a period of transition in punctuation practice. Elizabethan punctuation was much less a feature of the grammatical level than of rhythm and rhetoric, perhaps pointing to how a line should be scanned, or throwing into relief such figures as parallelism, antithesis and other balanced figures of speech. Full-stops sometimes bracketed what Mindele Treip, my chief guide in this field, calls 'rhythmical periods', which may well cluster together several grammatical sentences. Although by the second quarter of the century the movement towards modern practice of using punctuation as an aspect of the grammatical level was well underway, progress was by no means uniform, and Milton's own predilections would seem decidedly atavistic. The manuscript of *Paradise Lost* Book I shows a preference for light, rhythmical pointing, combined with the rhetorical use of emphatic, heavy pointing in places we should not expect it, such as around epic similes. Milton's printers tended to bring the manuscript punctuation into line with changing practice, but they did not effect the process uniformly, and many readings characteristic of MS Book I survive throughout the 1667 edition. Since punctuation reflects the interaction of printing-house convention and the habits of the author (and, conceivably, his amanuenses), we should not expect internal consistency, nor value it as a definitive guide to sentence divisions.[5]

In pulling out sentences for my study, then, I have used other criteria to determine where one ends and another begins. I consider a unit of text to be a sentence if it is grammatically complete, can be terminated without leaving grammatically incomplete fragments in residue and makes good sense. The final semantic requirement introduces a certain theoretical inelegance, in that it invokes the semantic level in analysis of syntax, and it points, too, to the inevitable introduction of a certain limited subjectivity and the possibilities for disagreement. In some cases, a semantic criterion must be invoked. Most difficulties reside in determining where to divide series of clausal units between which conjunctions may have been deleted. In some cases, different readers apply the criterion variously. Consider the following rather tricky example (the edition used preserves the punctuation of the 1674 edition, which generally follows that of 1667 and does so exactly here):

> So saying, her rash hand in evil hour
> Forth reaching to the fruit, she plucked, she ate:

Earth felt the wound, and nature from her seat
Sighing through all her works gave signs of woe,
That all was lost.

(*PL*, IX.780–4)

The sentence which begins 'So saying' may be perceived as stopping at one of at least three places. Some may feel that it should stop after 'plucked'. The participial phrases relating to 'saying' and 'reaching' define only the process of plucking, not of eating, and again, if 'she plucked' and 'she ate' are co-ordinated, we may perhaps have expected the deletion of the second identical conjunct, 'she'. Others could argue that the sentence ends at 'ate' and that the structure perhaps simulates a classical asyndeton. Others again would favour regarding the whole quotation as one long, co-ordinated sentence, in which the action is syntactically incorporated with its consequence. Each argument has some force, and only with hesitation did I choose between them (in fact, in favour of the first and earliest termination).

Such examples, fortunately, are fairly rare within the sample, but inevitably some elements of subjectivity from time to time occur in the process, in effect, of repunctuating the texts, nor is the problem unique to Milton.

Length and Complexity

Sentence length may be variously conceptualized, for example in terms of the average number of words per sentence, or the average number of syllables, or the average number of clauses. On each of these criteria, the Miltonic average is higher than that of the control group, though it does not distinguish him from all his contemporaries and the Milton oeuvre admits of important variations.

Table 2.1 expresses the overall information about sentence length. Already some aspects of Milton's practice appear quite sharply differentiated. On average Milton's sentences exceed the norms which emerge in the selected anthology and even more sharply exceed those of the whole control sample. The average Miltonic sentence contains roughly 28 per cent more words, 35

Table 2.1   Sentence length: overall information

Text	Number of words	Number of syllables	Number of clauses
PL	24.6	31.6	3.6
PR	26.0	34.5	4.2
Comus	29.2	38.0	3.9
SA	22.0	29.2	3.5
Milton's minor poems	18.9	24.0	2.6
Miltonic average	23.6	31.0	3.7
JACP	19.0	23.3	3.1
Civil War	12.6	15.1	1.8
Lusiads	28.0	36.7	4.3
Ann. Mir.	21.7	27.3	3.1
Non-Miltonic average	18.5	22.9	2.9

per cent more syllables and 28 per cent more clauses than the average for the whole non-Miltonic sample. That they should differ more sharply with respect to syllable content than to word content reflects a Miltonic penchant for longer words. However, we may surmise, in the absence of empirical information, that the reader's perception of sentence length and response to the demands it imposes are likely to be shaped by the quantities of both words and syllables, as well as by more complex aspects of linguistic practice, such as the quantity, kind and organization of the clausal structure.

These aspects of Milton's minor poems more closely resemble the norms of non-Miltonic practice, obviously a point to which we shall have to return later in this chapter. Similarly, Fanshawe in a sense out-Miltons Milton, and Dryden approaches the ranges of the Miltonic data, so we must be careful not to attribute too much weight to length alone as a major discriminant.

It is not simply that the typical Milton sentence is longer than a typical non-Miltonic one. The distribution of long and short sentences between Milton and the control group exhibits significant differences, as we may see from tables 2.2, 2.3, and 2.4. Milton has only marginally fewer sentences with less than ten

Table 2.2   Sentence length: words per sentence

Number of words per sentence	Milton		Non-Miltonic sample	
	Number of sentences	%	Number of sentences	%
1–9	116	24.5	79	25.7
10–19	144	30.4	135	44.0
20–29	83	17.5	41	13.4
30–39	61	12.9	33	10.7
40–49	25	5.3	9	2.9
50 or more	44	9.3	10	3.3

Chi-square 24.59987 with 5 d.f.; significance 0.0002.

Table 2.3   Sentence length: syllables per sentence

Number of syllables per sentence	Milton		Non-Miltonic sample	
	Number of sentences	%	Number of sentences	%
1–9	59	12.5	34	11.1
10–19	118	24.9	93	30.3
20–29	105	22.2	105	34.2
30–39	61	12.9	22	7.2
40–49	52	11.0	37	12.1
50 or more	78	16.5	16	5.2

Chi-square 37.81401 with 5 d.f.; significance 0.0000.

words than the control group, and marginally more with less than ten syllables. What really sets him apart is the high incidence of very long sentences. Roughly 16 per cent of his sentences have over fifty syllables; roughly 9 per cent have over fifty words; the average for contemporary, situationally analogous practice is roughly 5 and 3 per cent respectively. About 18 per cent of his sentences contain more than five clauses, compared with 10 per cent for the control group. It is not simply that Milton generates

Table 2.4 Sentence length: clauses per sentence

Number of clauses per sentence	Milton		Non-Miltonic sample	
	Number of sentences	%	Number of sentences	%
1	112	23.7	86	28.0
2	112	23.7	81	26.4
3	66	14.0	49	16.0
4	55	11.6	40	13.0
5	43	9.1	20	6.5
6–10	64	13.5	27	8.8
11 or more	21	4.4	4	1.3

Chi-square 13.56170 with 6 d.f.; significance 0.0349.

twenty-three-word sentences while those around are writing eighteen-word ones. Milton produces roughly the same proportion of very short sentences, rather fewer middling ones than contemporaries, and very considerably more that are substantially longer than the average. Indeed, within the Milton sample, I found fifteen examples of sentences of more than 100 syllables and six with more than 100 words, compared with only one sentence among contempories. Both the very short and the very long repay closer examination.

Short Sentences and Short Words

Milton's shorter sentences are characterized by the high incidence of monosyllabic words, as we may see from table 2.5. In general, there is a tendency for shorter words to predominate more strongly in shorter sentences, possibly as a natural trait of style: those same objectives, perhaps of simplicity or pithiness or even an epigrammatic or lapidary turn, which may prompt a poet to a sentence of few words may well prompt him to eschew the polysyllabic and select monosyllables. The manoeuvre works especially well among devotional writers, where brevity may

Table 2.5 Word length: average number of syllables per word

	Average word length (in syllables)	
	Milton	Non-Miltonic
Sentences of less than 10 syllables	1.238	1.227
Sentences of 10 or more syllables	1.317	1.244
All sentences	1.307	1.242

serve a decorum of vatic sublimity. George Herbert sometimes achieves a transcendent simplicity that stands out even from the plain texture of his poetry. Consider the force of the concluding refrain in 'The Quip':

> Then came quick Wit and Conversation,
> And he would needs a comfort be,
> And, to be short, make an oration.
> But thou shalt answer, Lord, for me.
>   (*JACP*, p. 115)

The poem develops a contrast between the seductive entanglements of worldliness and the ineffable resolve of the faithful. The good Christian has no answer to the enticements of beauty, money, wit and glory: he can merely refer them to God for his final judgement. The style of 'But thou . . . for me' works to suggest something of the paradox of inarticulate sublimity.

Herbert's less illustrious imitator, Ralph Knevet, produces a similar use of the brief and monosyllabic to effect textural and thematic contrast in the concluding couplets of 'The Passion':

> But I am whelmed in sorrows and in fears,
> Because I cannot drown my sins in tears.
>   What shall I say?
>   I thus will pray:
> As blood and water issued from thy wound,
> So with thy blood, do Thou my tears compound.
>   (*JACP*, p. 249)

The monosyllablic expression of 'What shall I say?' and of the
ensuing clause, which completes the couplet, contrasts lightly
with what comes before and after. The turn of the argument,
from the convolution of 'But I . . . in tears' to the resolution of
the final couplet is effected through the terse interrogative.

The distinction among non-Miltonic writers between the average word length in very short sentences and that in the rest of the
sample is rather less pronounced than in the case of Milton,
whose use of short and predominantly monosyllabic sentences
achieves a variety of quite telling local effects. Consider the
following from his apprentice-piece, 'On the Death of a Fair
Infant Dying of a Cough':

> So mounting up in icy-pearled car,
> Through middle empire of the freezing air
> He wandered long, till thee he spied from far,
> There ended was his quest, there ceased his care.
>   (lines 15–18)

The passage, which describes the quest of 'Bleak winter' for a
fitting spouse, shows a delicate sensitivity to the expressive potential of syntactic variation. The sentence 'So mounting . . . spied
from far' exhibits a certain complexity of clausal structure, and it
has an inversion ('thee he spied'), five disyllabic words and the
four-syllabled neologism 'icy-pearled', characteristics which perhaps suit well the arduousness of the venture they describe, and
which contrast with the finality expressed in and perhaps implied
by the terse monosyllables of the two syntactically discrete units,
'There . . . quest' and 'there ceased his care'.

The use of such sentences to suggest vatic enigma can be seen
in Milton's adaptation of the Pauline 'When all things shall be
subdued unto him, then shall the Son also himself be subject unto
him that put all things under him, that God may be all in all' (1
Cor. 15:28):

> Then thou thy regal sceptre shalt lay by,
> For regal sceptre then no more shall need,
> God shall be all in all.
>   (PL, III.339–41)

Milton severs the syntactic connection between 'God . . . in all', which for the purposes of this exercise we may regard as a discrete sentence, and the predictions that Christ's sceptre shall be laid by. What Paul means is not really any easier to fix than what Milton means, but in Paul, or at least in the translation of the Authorized Version, the conclusion is offered as if premissed on 'When all things . . . under him'. Contrarily, Milton does nothing to accommodate God's utterance to the limitations of human understanding. In the paradox of simplicity and complexity, 'God shall be all in all' resonates, oracular, riddling, profound.

Much of Milton's poetry relates in various ways to the representation of human speech. *Comus* is a masque, *Samson Agonistes* has the formal characteristics of a drama, and very many sections of his epics take the form of dialogue, debate, soliloquy, address, monologue, etc. I shall consider later in more general terms how such considerations may inform the texture of his verse. The dramatic use of short, markedly monosyllabic sentences may be remarked on here.

Consider the brevity of those sentences which conclude this speech of Manoa:

> I have attempted one by one the lords,
> Either at home, or through the high street passing,
> With supplication prone and father's tears
> To accept of ransom for my son their prisoner,
> Some much averse I found and wondrous harsh,
> Contemptuous, proud, set on revenge and spite;
> That part more reverenced Dagon and his priests,
> Others more moderate seeming, but their aim
> Private reward, for which both god and state
> They easily would set to sale, a third
> More generous far and civil, who confessed
> They had enough revenged, having reduced
> Their foe to misery beneath their fears,
> The rest was magnanimity to remit,
> If some convenient ransom were proposed.
> What noise or shout was that? It tore the sky.
> (*SA*, lines 1457–72)

The speech is part of the 120 lines between the departure of

Samson and the entry of the Messenger with his account of the
destruction of the Philistian temple, a passage wholly occupied by
a dialogue between Manoa and the Hebrew Chorus. A powerfully dramatic schema informs the scene, as savage events off-
stage break into and finally overwhelm rational discussion. In this
passage, Manoa describes his guileful lobbying in language of
some syntactic complexity, which permits the careful qualification
with which he distinguishes the variety of Philistian response to
his approaches. The stark interrogative and the terse 'It tore the
sky' interrupt the patient and detailed exposition as a brutal
intrusion of a reality much simpler than Manoa's improbable
politicking. The passage surely owes much of its effectiveness to
the sudden shift in syntactic structure.

Elsewhere, brevity of sentence length serves another dramatic
decorum, that of bluntness. It often characterizes the way in
which the godly address Satan and his cohorts. Thus, at the outset
of the revolt in Heaven, Abdiel, the solitary angel under Satan's
command who resists his leader, steps forward to confront him in
a speech which begins, 'Proud, art thou met?' (*PL*, VI.131).
Again, Eve, while she is still capable of a moral response to the
serpent's blandishments, begins her response to the specious
disclosure that eating the fruit has given the animal the faculty of
speech with the frank though perhaps rather bewildered question, 'What may this mean?' (*PL*, IX.553).

A particularly good example comes from late in *Paradise
Regained*. Satan has aggravated the horrors of a stormy night by
releasing 'Infernal ghosts, and hellish furies' and 'grisly spectres'
to taunt Christ (IV.422, 430), and the next day approaches him
with an elaborate and decorously phrased enquiry into whether
the events of the night have deterred him from his mission: 'Fair
morning yet betides thee Son of God, / After a dismal night'
(IV.451–2). Christ responds with no gesture of courtesy:

> the Son of God went on
> And stayed not, but in brief him answered thus.
> Me worse than wet thou find'st not;
> (IV.484–6)

The passage works well for the modern reader, but consider how much more striking it would have been for a contemporary audience attuned to the grandiloquent civilities of formal address. Such formality is simulated in much of the dialogue in Milton's writing. We find it both in the insidious politeness of treacherous figures, as shown by Comus (lines 264–9) or Satan (*PL*, IX.532–6), and in the ways in which the godly speak to each other, as in Adam's address to Eve (IV.411–12) or Eve's to Adam (IV.440–2). These curt approaches are the more forthright because of what is missing, the terms of respectful address that characterize polite exchanges.

Longer Sentences and Complexity of Sentence Structure

A high proportion of Milton's sentences are more than twice the average length for sentences within his oeuvre: 9.3 per cent have fifty or more words, 16.5 per cent fifty or more syllables and 9.5 per cent eight or more clauses of all kinds. For the control group, the respective figures are 3.3, 5.2, and 2.9 per cent, significantly lower than Milton's. The operations of his longer sentences are not straightforward, nor may they usefully be detached from a wider consideration of the clausal complexity which characterizes Milton's syntax.

Despite the comparative length of his sentences, Milton shows no pronounced predilection for the co-ordinated conjunction of main clauses. On average, each sentence within the Milton sample contains 1.45 main clauses, and within the control sample 1.40 – not the sort of distinction which contributes much to the differentiation of poetic texture. Similarly, 66.2 per cent of the sentences in the Miltonic sample and 66.4 per cent of those from the control group contain only one main clause; the trifling distinction, of course, is of no statistical significance. Milton's longer sentences (that is, those containing more than fifty words) seem likelier to contain more than one main clause, though again the results are of low statistical significance, and unsurprisingly the average number of main clauses is a little higher in such sentences (1.64) than in shorter ones (1.43). If we restrict our computation only to those sentences which have more than fifty words, a higher proportion of non-Miltonic sentences have two or more main clauses than we find in Milton, but the subsample for the control group is small and the findings of low statistical significance. In the non-Miltonic group, between long and short sentences the distinction in the average number of main clauses is much sharper (2.0, as opposed to 1.38), though we must recall the caveat that numbers of examples of long sentences are very small.

We may conclude with some confidence that the co-ordination of main clauses is not a major feature of Miltonic syntax and that it neither distinguishes him from contemporary norms nor explains the processes which particularly characterize the generation of his longer sentences, though, obviously, longer sentences do contain more main clauses on average.

Significant distinctions do, however, emerge in the matter of subordination (table 2.6). Within the sample, a higher proportion of Miltonic sentences contain at least one subordinate clause. (For the purposes of this part of the investigation, participial phrases are categorized as subordinate clauses.) On average, in the Milton sample there are, for every main clause, 0.87 subordinate clauses; in the non-Miltonic texts, the average figure is 0.77. My earlier investigation into the characteristics of Milton's prose style identified what I termed 'multibranching' as a recurrent and, to some extent, distinctive feature of his writing; that is, quite a high proportion of main clauses in Milton's prose support a plurality of subordinate clauses dependent directly upon them.[6] Certainly we find such constructions in his poetic oeuvre, as in Satan's report to his fellows of the success of his mission:

> he [God] thereat
> Offended, worth your laughter, hath given up
> Both his beloved man and all this world,
> To Sin and Death a prey, and so to us,
> Without our hazard, labour, or alarm,
> To range in, and to dwell, and over man
> To rule, as over all he should have ruled.
> (*PL*, x.487–93)

This is a complex sentence, over fifty words long, made trickier by the high incidence of appositional and prepositional phrases.

Table 2.6 Subordination: overall information

Number of subordinate clauses per sentence	Milton		Non-Miltonic sample	
	Number of sentences	%	Number of sentences	%
0	158	33.4	124	40.4
1 or more	315	66.6	183	59.6

Chi-square 3.64049 with 1 d.f.; significance 0.0564.

The main clause, 'he . . . hath given up . . . man and all this world', supports within it the participial 'thereat offended' and ends with the cluster of directly subordinate clauses 'To range . . . to dwell . . . To rule'. But I found fewer such structures than my experience of his prose had led me to expect. Sentences containing three or four or more subordinate clauses dependent directly on the main clause or clauses are scarcely more common in Milton than in the writers of the control group, as we may see from table 2.7, from which sentences containing no subordination have been excluded.

What does offer a sharp distinction between Milton and his contemporaries is the high incidence in the former of what we may term 'lower subordination', that is, of subordinate clauses which depend, not directly on main clauses, but on clauses which are themselves subordinate. In Milton, the average incidence of such clauses is 0.95 per sentence; in the control group, it is 0.42. In Milton, the average incidence of such clauses for each clause which is directly dependent on a main clause is 0.75; in the control group, 0.40. A significantly higher proportion of Milton's sentences contain such clauses (30.7 per cent, compared to 22.5 per cent of the sentences of the non-Miltonic group). More remarkably still, Milton generates quite a high proportion of sentences with a plurality of such clauses, as we may see from table 2.8. Within the non-Miltonic sample, only two sentences have more than four clauses which depend, not on a main clause, but on clauses which are themselves subordinate (from Richard Crashaw, 'An Apology for the Foregoing Hymn', and Henry

Table 2.7 Plurality of subordination

Number of subordinate clauses directly dependent on a main clause	Milton		Non-Miltonic sample	
	Number of sentences	%	Number of sentences	%
1	163	51.7	98	53.6
2	79	25.1	51	27.9
3	41	13.0	21	11.5
4 or more	32	10.2	13	7.1

Chi-square 1.83319 with 3 d.f.; significance 0.6077.

Table 2.8 Lower subordination

Number of clauses dependent on other subordinate clauses per sentence	Milton		Non-Miltonic sample	
	Number of sentences	%	Number of sentences	%
0	328	69.3	238	77.5
1	58	12.3	40	13.0
2	26	5.5	13	4.2
3 or more	61	12.9	16	5.2

Chi-square 13.53389 with 3 d.f.; significance 0.0036.

Vaughan, 'The Retreat'). More than 2 per cent of sentences in the Milton sample have five such clauses, and several have eight or nine. There are even a couple of examples of sentences with fifteen such clauses. Both are from *Paradise Lost*, and both are sentences of over 100 words and a score of clauses in total. Milton's poetic practice here resembles closely a principal characteristic of his prose. There, however, it distinguished him less sharply from what was typical among contemporary exponents of the same genre; among poets, Milton seems unique.

We are close, I think, to unlocking the process by which Milton characteristically generates the long sentences which so mark his style. Typically, they are not produced by a predilection for the compounding of main clauses. Rather, they originate in a slightly higher incidence of subordinate clauses dependent on main clauses combined with a much higher incidence of clauses dependent on material which is itself subordinate.

The basic model admits an almost infinite variety of structural alternatives and of effect. At perhaps its simplest, clause supports clause, which supports clause, down a long chain of dependency. Consider:

A
[he through heaven,
B
[That opened wide her blazing portals,] led
A
To God's eternal house direct the way,
C
A broad and ample road,] [whose dust is gold
C   D
And pavement stars,] [as stars to thee appear,]
E
[Seen in the galaxy, that Milky Way]
F
[Which nightly as a circling zone thou seest]
G
[Powdered with stars.]

(*PL*, VII.574–81)

A certain element of syntactic ambiguity adheres to all such complex structures, but the relationship of clause to clause may probably most naturally be represented as in figure 2.1. Here Raphael describes to Adam the process of earth's creation and Christ's triumph at its accomplishment. The explanation he develops works towards the reconstitution of celestial events in terms tractable to Adam's understanding. Detail is glossed by detail, which is glossed by detail till the road Christ travelled is equated with that which Adam may nightly see, the stars of the Milky Way, and the schema of gradual elucidation accords well with the syntactical pattern. Thus, in one of the more straightforward models for sentences of such proportions, clause supports clause, which supports clause, through a long chain of subordination and elucidation, as the angel adjusts the transcendent to man's comprehension. The account begins with the blazing portals of

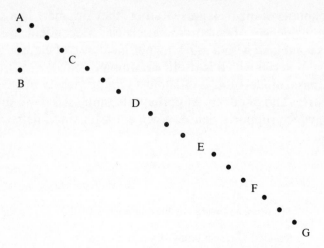

Figure 2.1   *PL*, VII.574–81: clausal structure

heaven and ends with the almost homely metaphor of the sky
'powdered' with stars: mere dust, that which is familiar to man, is
presented at the end of a long construction that has worked to
bring the transcendent within the scope of human comprehension. Raphael (and, indirectly, Milton) had expressed frequent
anxiety about describing 'what surmounts the reach / Of human
sense' (*PL*, V.571–2; see also, for example, VI.296–301): the
tenuous but perseverant syntax admirably suits the assiduity of
the account.

The next example shows a radically different organizing strategy
within the options presented by the kinds of complexity we have
analysed:

```
                              B
                   [As when a prowling wolf,
              D                      G
      [Whom hunger drives] [to seek new haunt for prey,]
          E                          H
      [Watching] [where shepherds pen their flocks at eve
                              H
      In hurdled cotes amid the field secure,]
                              B
      Leaps o'er the fence with ease into the fold:]
              C                   F
      [Or as a thief bent [to unhoard the cash
```

```
          F                       I
Of some rich burgher,] [whose substantial doors,
    J              K            I
[Cross-barred] and [bolted fast,] fear no assault,]
              C
In at the window climbs, or o'er the tiles;]
              A
[So clomb this first grand thief into God's fold] [.]
                                    (PL, IV.183–92)
```

The passage describes Satan's entry into the garden of Eden in terms which, as has been recognized, perform a number of thematic and rhetorical functions. The extended similes, likening him in turn to a wolf and a thief, function perhaps as part of that narrative degradation of Satan which Waldock speaks of.[7] Again, Satan is linked as archetype to ectype: the thief and the wolf (or at least the postlapsarian wolf – before the Fall, they were vegetarian, we presume) repeat the Edenic crimes of Satan.[8] That others follow on where Satan led is confirmed by Milton's next sentence, of a blunt finality, which builds on Paul's caveat of Acts 21: 28–9: 'So since into his church lewd hirelings climb' (line 193). The most coherent interpretation of the relationship of the constituent clauses can be seen in figure 2.2. Once more, the complex syntax achieves considerable literary impact. We have in the two epic similes, as such figures are traditionally called, two brief yet detailed narratives of events that are complete in their depiction of causality and effect. The touchstones for Satanic conduct (in typological terms, its types, and, in historical terms, its consequences) are imaginatively realized before the reader is led to make the proper connection with the 'Author of evil' (PL, VI.262). The thief and the wolf and (by implication the minister) are held in syntactic subordination to Satan, to whom they extend moral subordination.

My final example, rather more complex than the former two, discloses all the power and beauty of Milton's syntactic control:

```
              A
      [so shall the world go on,
              A
To good malignant, to bad men benign,]
```

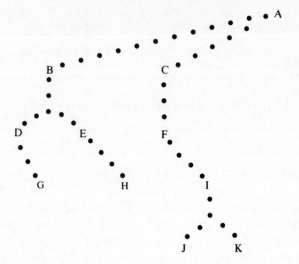

Figure 2.2   *PL*, IV.183–92: clausal structure

          B   C
[Under her own weight groaning] [till the day
               C
Appear of respiration to the just,
               C
And vengeance to the wicked, at return
        C   D
Of him] [so lately promised to thy aid
        D   E
The woman's seed,] [obscurely then foretold,]
               F
[Now amplier known thy saviour and thy Lord,]
               G
[Last in the clouds from heaven to be revealed
        G   H
In glory of the Father,] [to dissolve
        H   I
Satan with his perverted world,] [then raise
        I   J   K
From the conflagrant mass, [purged] and [refined,]
               I
New heavens, new earth, ages of endless date]
               L
[Founded in righteousness and peace and love]
               M
[To bring forth fruits joy and eternal bliss.]
                             (*PL*, XII.537–51)

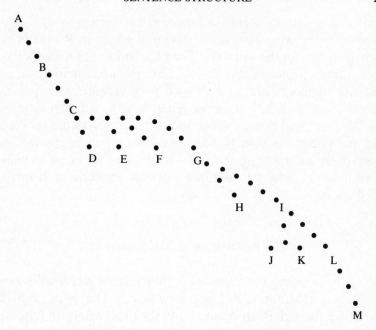

Figure 2.3 *PL*, XII.537–51: clausal structure

The sentence concludes Michael's long account of mankind's prospects in the fallen world – for the most part, a gloomy narrative, though it ends with the triumphant vision of Christ's redemption and the millennium. The structure is formally gratifying, as figure 2.3 discloses. At each level of subordination, clauses cluster, but only the last acts as a node for further dependent material: thus, C supports D, E, F and G; G supports H and I; I supports J, K and L; and L supports M. The organizing principle appears to operate more freely than the parallelism that has sometimes been remarked on in the study of seventeenth-century prose,[9] as surge follows surge in the relentless tide of Michael's vision. The reader's concentration, taxed to its limit, struggles towards that final clause, dependent as it is, at sixth remove, on the main clause with which the sentence opened: 'To bring forth fruits joy and eternal bliss.' As Fowler observes, 'fruits' echoes the opening lines of the poem, 'Of man's first disobedience, and the fruit / Of that forbidden tree',[10] and 'fruit(s)', in both its literal and more metaphorical significations, recurs in interesting ways throughout the poem, as Ricks notes.[11] Here it occurs for the last time. The final fruits of that disobedient fruit-eating, primarily thanks to Christ's atonement, but secondarily thanks to the godly's own perseverance, are 'joy and eternal bliss', but they are achieved at length and after struggle, much as that final clause, which so fittingly resolves the problems that the poem has posed, is vouchsafed only after the reader's comprehension has struggled through. Perhaps we begin to understand how and why the sentence works to produce such intense satisfaction.

The Positioning of Main Clauses

As we have seen, questions of Latinity have historically been raised about Milton's sentence structure.[12] The issue must be addressed, though its translation into the problematic of linguistic stylistics makes its resolution likelier and elevates the debate above mere rhetoric.

Does Milton in some ways uncharacteristic of seventeenth-century poetry so order his sentences that the main clause is persistently interrupted or postponed? Table 2.9 presents an analysis of those subordinate clauses which depend directly on main clauses. I categorize them as 'left-branching' (that is, occurring before the main clause), 'right-branching' (after the main clause') or 'embedded' (located within the main clause). Evidently, though there are differences of emphasis – Milton favours the embedded clause rather more than left-branching constructions – he is not sharply distinguished from his contemporaries by any pronounced predilection for concluding sentences with main clauses rather than subordinate ones. On average, a Miltonic sentence contains 0.26 embedded subclauses, 0.15 left-branching clauses and 0.88 right-branching subclauses; for his contemporaries, the corresponding figures are 0.17, 0.17 and 0.73. Most certainly, Milton is not likelier than the generality of other poets to conclude complex sentences with the main clause, as we may see from table 2.10, which is based upon an analysis of those

Table 2.9   The position of subordinate clauses: overall information

Subordinate clause	Milton		Non-Miltonic sample	
	Number of clauses	%	Number of clauses	%
Embedded	122	20.1	52	15.8
Right-branching	414	68.3	223	68.0
Left-branching	70	11.6	53	16.2

Table 2.10   The incidence of right-branching clauses

	Milton		Non-Miltonic sample	
	Number	%	Number	%
Nothing after main clause	62	19.4	39	21.3
Right-branching clause	257	80.6	144	78.7

Chi-square 0.15125 with 1 d.f.; significance 0.6973.

sentences within the samples that have at least one subordinate clause.

Certainly we find examples of sentences ending in main clauses, such as the elaborate construction from *Paradise Lost*, IV.183–92, which we considered above, sprinkled through the Milton oeuvre and the work of contemporaries, though few are so complex, and sentences with more than five constituent clauses are quite rare. I note only four in all the Milton sample and two from among his contemporaries.

Plainly, the concept of Latinity embraces larger and vaguer aspects of style than the sorts of postponement which may seem reminiscent of Latin periodic constructions. On that narrow aspect, however, we may be clear: Milton plays no such mannered games with his readers, and his sentences develop through subordination, left-branching, right-branching and embedded, as seems appropriate to the expressive demands of the moment. Syntactically, Milton dances to a thoroughly English tune.

Narrative and Non-narrative Modes in *Paradise Lost*

Several of Milton's poems consist of a mixture of modes of discourse, and *Paradise Lost* is sufficiently large to admit easy analysis of stylistic markers of the various constituents. I begin with the largest distinction, that between those sections of the poem which are narrative and those which simulate speech or else (a small group) are invocatory. For these purposes, I have regarded as narrative those speeches in which Raphael describes the war in heaven and the Creation and Michael offers Adam a vision of the course of world history after the Fall (in *PL*, V–VIII and XI–XII).

The characteristic sentences of narrative and non-narrative discourse may seem superficially quite similar. On average, narrative sentences are a little longer, in terms of syllables and in words though they have fewer clauses (table 2.11). In both kinds of discourse, however, Miltonic practice remains quite sharply distinguished from the non-Miltonic norms (see table 2.1). Several rather subtler distinctions, however, obtain.

Very short sentences are much more a feature of the non-narrative sections. Sentences of less than ten syllables are more than four times more common in those sections of the poem which simulate speech or issue invocations (table 2.12). As is true of the Milton oeuvre in general, these short sentences are usually characterized by short words. While those in speech may serve all the expressive functions available to those in narrative, they have, as I have suggested, something of a dramatic potential. They may embody expressions of an imperative, interrogative or declarative kind. Hence Christ's words to God the Father: 'on me let thine anger fall' (*PL*, III.237); or Satan's puzzled question to himself, about the tree of knowledge: 'Can it be death [to know]?' (IV.518); or Adam's response to Eve's reproach for letting her work alone and so exposing her to Satan's guile: 'what could I more?' (IX.1170).

Table 2.11   Sentence length in *PL* (narrative and non-narrative
modes): overall information

Mode of discourse	Number of words	Number of syllables	Number of clauses
Narrative	24.4	32.8	3.5
Non-narrative	23.7	30.8	3.9

Table 2.12   Sentence length in *PL* (narrative and non-narrative
modes): syllables per sentence

Number of syllables per sentence	Narrative mode		Non-narrative mode	
	Number of sentences	%	Number of sentences	%
1–9	5	4.4	31	19.3
10 or more	109	95.6	130	80.7

Chi-square 11.69510 with 1 d.f.; significance 0.0006.

Speeches in Milton's epics are remote from the syntax and
vocabulary of everyday mid-seventeenth-century conversation, in
so far as we may reasonably guess at those norms. We have, so far
as I am aware, no direct evidence in the form of unmediated
transcriptions of such dialogue, but it is, of course, absurd to
imagine it to have been characterized by the sorts of trait we find
in Milton. Modern oral modes of discourse – even quite structured kinds – are sharply differentiated from written modes: we
may suppose that similar markers contemporaneously obtained.
Yet in the high incidence of short sentences, we have one formal
differentiation, inscribed in the fabric of the poetry, of differences
in discourse. Milton is not naturalistically simulating how men
and women (and God and his angels, for that matter) speak: but
he is formally marking off some parts of his poem as the (poetic,
elevated, epic) representation of dialogue.

His narrative sections have approximately the same proportion
of sentences of twice the average length as do the other parts of

Table 2.13 Plurality of main clauses in *PL* (narrative and
non-narrative modes)

Number of main clauses per sentence	Narrative mode		Non-narrative mode	
	Number of sentences	%	Number of sentences	%
1	64	56.1	116	72.0
2 or more	50	43.9	45	28.0

Chi-square 6.78385 with 1 d.f.; significance 0.0092.

the poem. There are, however, other markers. Narrative sentences are much likelier to have a plurality of main clauses (table 2.13). Sometimes, such sentences have three or four main clauses, each relatively simple, supporting no subordinate clauses or else perhaps just one. Such structures serve elegantly the plain exposition of serial events linked primarily by their temporal relationship rather than by notions of causality or conditionality. Thus, after God the Father has asked for volunteers to atone for man's sin, Milton adds:

> He asked, but all the heavenly choir stood mute,
> And silence was in heaven[.]
>
> (III.217–18)

Such structures are to be found again in Michael's prophetic narrative of postlapsarian history, as in his account of Noah:

> At length a reverend sire among them came,
> And of their doings great dislike declared,
> And testified against their ways[.]
>
> (XI.719–21)

The style accords well with the brevity of the historical vignettes of Michael's account: history is witnessed by Adam as if he were watching a pageant or dumbshow, in which issues of motivation or processes of ratiocination are not addressed. But the simple structure of main-clause co-ordination can, on occasion, carry considerable expressive weight. Consider Adam's response to judgement:

> on the ground
> Outstretched he lay, on the cold ground, and oft
> Cursed his creation, death as oft accused
> Of tardy execution, since denounced
> The day of his offence.
>
>   (x.850–4)

This sentence presents several minor variants from usual syntactic practice. The deletion of the co-ordinating conjunction between 'creation' and 'death' puzzles the reader. So, too, the inversion of 'death . . . accused', which brings 'death' and 'creation' into such stark adjacency. The reiteration, 'on the ground . . . on the cold ground', seems disturbingly redundant. The ellipsis of 'since denounced / The day of his offence' compels us to labour to supply what is missing: 'since [it was] denounced [i.e. announced] [on] the day of his offence', I suppose, but what was denounced, 'death' or the 'execution' of death? The text needs working at. Is it fanciful, I wonder, to see in the structuring of this curiously problematic sentence a form mimetic of the agitation of Adam, returning, profitlessly, to what he has experienced and labouring to supply to his reason what he cannot know?

Other major aspects of clausal structure distinguish narrative from non-narrative discourse. On average, each main clause in the narrative sections supports 0.76 subordinate clauses; in the non-narrative parts, it is a little higher, 0.87, though sentences without any subordination are not significantly higher in the narrative sections. The non-narrative sections are much more sharply distinguished by the high incidence of subordinate clauses which depend, not directly on main clauses, but on other subordinate material. In the narrative sections, the average subordinate clause dependent on a main clause supports 0.67 dependent clauses: in the non-narrative sections the figure is almost double, 1.10. Significantly more sentences in the non-narrative sections manifest clauses of this type (table 2.14). Now we have come to recognize that sentences containing such structures are features which distinguish Miltonic syntax quite sharply from the general

Table 2.14   Lower subordination in *PL* (narrative and non-
narrative modes)

Number of subordinate clauses dependent on other subordinate clauses per sentence	Narrative mode		Non-narrative mode	
	Number of sentences	%	Number of sentences	%
0	83	72.8	100	62.1
1 or more	31	27.2	61	37.9

Chi-square 2.96570 with 1 d.f.; significance 0.0850.

run of mid-seventeenth-century poetic practice. It would seem that this aspect of style further distinguishes those sections of *Paradise Lost* which simulate oral registers of discourse from the narrative sections. The speeches in Milton are in one sense more distinctively Miltonic than the sections that set the scene and relate the story.

Speeches in *Paradise Lost* frequently function as vehicles not for conversation but for oratory, in both its epideictic and disputational modes, for praises to and invocations of the Almighty and his agents, and for open debate, for controversy, and for the specious arguments of seducers. Critics have from time to time remarked upon the similarity between some of the discussion of issues in *Paradise Lost* and in Milton's controversial prose.[13] We should not, perhaps, be surprised that the poetic discourse in such contexts should exhibit quite sharply one of the more distinctive characteristics of Miltonic prose, its high incidence of subordinate material which in turn depends on other subordinate clauses. Such structures serve well the ends of complex argument, and surely one of the distinctions of Miltonic poetry is that his characters do argue seriously about complex issues. The most heroic exchanges in Miltonic epic are always essentially intellectual, battles of minds not physical tussles. The complex structures I have identified permit the representation of controversy, allow the expression of reservations, qualifications, explanations, and admit arguments to be pressed through skeins of subordination to ultimate conviction or confutation. Milton's extraordinary ca-

pacity to absorb such elements into the texture of his epic constitutes one of the finest achievements of his poetic art and enables
him to address issues of great theological and ethical complexity.

Lineation and Syntax

Milton's minor poetry, generally distinct from his longer works,
conforms for the most part to prosodic models other than the
iambic pentameter which elsewhere predominates in his poetic
oeuvre, and so I have excluded it from this discussion. I consider
it, of a piece, a little later. I have further restricted my account of
the Cain anthology to sentences which at least begin and end in
ten-syllabled lines.

Milton's practice in organizing the arrangement of sentences
within the ten-syllabled line may be distinguished generally from
the norms contemporaneously obtaining, and his practice in
Paradise Lost is singularly unusual. I categorized sentences into
three groups: those in which both beginning and end correspond
to a line division, that is, both ends are stopped at line breaks;
those in which either the beginning or the end corresponds to a
line break, what I term 'one end stopped'; and those in which the
beginning falls in a syllable other than the first in the line and the
end falls in a syllable other than the tenth and last, that is, neither
end is stopped at the line break. Table 2.15 discloses some
remarkable variations in practice. The distinctions are most marked
between Milton and the poems which are situationally closest to
his epics, *The Civil War*, *Annus Mirabilis* and *The Lusiads*. These
differ from each other quite considerably in terms of syntax and
prosody. Cowley's poem has very short sentences and is written
throughout in rhyming couplets. Dryden uses sentences of a
length quite similar to the Miltonic average in a poem in stanzaic
quatrains. Fanshawe's translation is in *ottava rima* and his average sentence is longer than Milton's. Yet each conforms to some
tacit formula by which the overwhelming majority of sentences
begin and end at line divisions, though with perhaps rather
different effects.

In Cowley, sentences are usually contained within couplets,

Table 2.15 Lineation and syntax

| | Type of sentence | | | | | |
| | Both ends stopped | | One end stopped | | Neither end stopped | |
	Number	%	Number	%	Number	%
PL	82	29.8	138	50.2	55	20.0
PR	26	49.1	21	39.6	6	11.3
Comus	11	52.4	7	33.3	3	14.3
SA	25	54.3	15	32.6	6	13.0
Lusiads	19	95.0	1	0.5	0	–
Civil War	63	88.7	8	11.3	0	–
Ann. Mir.	45	100.0	0	–	0	–
JACP	37	61.7	18	30.0	5	8.3

Chi-square 153.38959 with 14 d.f.; significance 0.0000.

and the poem reads rather like a series of discrete aphorisms sharing virtually the same rhythm and length and exhibiting little variation in sentence structure:

> It was not soe when the vast Fleete of *Spaine*
> Lay torne and scatter'd ore the injur'd *Maine*.
> Through the proud world a *Virgin* Terror strooke,
> The *Austrian* Crownes and *Romes* seaven *Hills* she shooke.
> To her great *Neptune* homag'd all his Streames,
> And all the wide strecht *Ocean* was her *Thames*.
> (*Civil War*, I.59–64)

It is difficult to see what advantages this format has for Cowley's purposes, which for the most part rest in the development of a rather tendentious narrative. The highly regular coincidence of sentence endings, line endings and the rhymes disjoints the relation of events. Issues which relate each to the other seemed sealed within their respective couplets.

Dryden and Fanshawe cope rather better with the implications of these stylistic choices, probably because the organizing prosodic unit is not the couplet but the stanza, and the rhyme scheme is less insistent. God witnesses the fire of London thus:

At length th'Almighty cast a pitying eye,
  And mercy softly touch'd his melting breast:
He saw the Town's one half in rubbish lie,
  And eager flames give on to storm the rest.
                    (*Ann. Mir.*, lines 1117–20)

The two sentences, 'At length . . . breast' and 'He saw . . . rest',
are cross-stitched by the rhyme scheme. The stanza seems to
function, almost as if it were a syntactic unit, and the ultimately
rather irksome bittiness of Cowley's epic is to some extent
avoided. The considerable complexities of Fanshawe's *ottava
rima* quite distract any consciousness of the high co-occurrence of
sentence-ends and line breaks.

Milton's practice defies generalization. Certainly, sentences
end or begin at line divisions at a rate that is far higher than it
would be were the positioning of sentences within the decasyllabic line purely random, and the coincidence of syntactic and
linear divisions surely functions as a major mechanism in the tacit
reassertion that his unrhymed pentameter remains formally distinguished from prose and significantly removed from the interpretative strategies and readerly expectations appropriate to
prose genres. I have identified no clear pattern in Milton's practice, however. There is no significant correlation between sentence length and end-stopping. It is not especially characteristic
of long sentences, of twice the average length, or of short sentences, of half the average length. Within *Paradise Lost*, end-
stopped sentences are as likely to occur in those sections which
represent speech as in the narrative parts. I suspect, though I
have not statistically confirmed, that Milton takes care to intro-
duce such sentences fairly regularly, as a reaffirmation of the
basic decasyllabic structure of his poetry. That he should do so
less frequently than his contemporaries – and especially so in
Paradise Lost – relates most directly to his generally freer notion
of the relationship between lineation and all syntactic structures,
down to the intraclausal level. I feel less confident in developing
explanations for the distinctions which obtain between *Paradise
Lost* and Milton's other long poems at this point.

The notion of a Miltonic caesura has frequently been explored.[14]
I prefer to leave aside those finer prosodic points which invoke

Table 2.16   Syllabic location of sentence divisions in *PL*

Location of sentence division	Number	%
Between syllables 1 and 2	0	–
2 and 3	12	4.8
3 and 4	24	10.1
4 and 5	58	23.4
5 and 6	36	14.6
6 and 7	75	30.3
7 and 8	25	10.1
8 and 9	16	6.4
9 and 10	1	0.4

rather subjective concepts of stress and emphasis, but certainly in the case of those sentences in the sample that terminate or begin within the line, rather than at its end, we have some evidence of Milton's preferences in the distribution of such inter-sentence pauses. Table 2.16 presents the information about *Paradise Lost*: sample sizes for the other poems are probably too small to allow much interpretation. The emphases in Miltonic practice are quite pronounced. Lines that are broken by sentence termination and inception tend to have those breaks towards the middle, though much less frequently between fifth and sixth syllables than between fourth and fifth or sixth and seventh. We may only speculate on the advantages Milton may have associated with the skewing of the line break. I find its effect rather elusive to demonstrate, though Milton's avoidance of the first and last possible slots within the lines may well serve some concept of a euphonious fluency.

Most poets of the mid-seventeenth century, it would seem, when they write sentences of more than one line in length, seem a little chary about breaking them at line endings within clausal structures: the line division more usually falls between clauses, and so corresponds to a major syntactic distinction. Most emphatically in *Paradise Lost*, but significantly so in *Paradise Regained* and *Samson Agonistes*, Milton breaks more often within clauses than between them (table 2.17), though for the first time we note an important distinction between the texture of *Comus* and his other long poems.

Table 2.17 Lineation and clausal division

	Line breaks between clauses		Line breaks within clauses	
	Number	%	Number	%
PL	188	26.4	525	73.6
PR	53	36.3	93	63.7
Comus	44	51.8	41	48.2
SA	45	38.8	85	61.2
Lusiads	32	59.3	22	41.7
Civil War	23	59.0	16	41.0
Ann. Mir.	57	73.1	21	26.9
JACP (pentameter only)	40	44.4	50	55.6

Milton's mature practice contrasts most sharply with that of the young Dryden. Just as the latter had begun and ended his sentences in *Annus Mirabilis* in step with the lineation, so too he generally has line ending correspond with clausal division. In Milton's later poetry, the relationship between syntax and prosodic division is less pronounced. Just as sentences, especially in *Paradise Lost*, begin or terminate with some frequency at places elsewhere in the line other than syllable one or syllable ten, so too the line endings fall within clauses more often than they fall between clauses.

How are we to interpret this pronounced stylistic trait? The status of line breaks in poetry has intermittently exercised theoreticians and prosodists down the ages.[15] It is sometimes argued that the line end functions as a pause or disjunction in the poetry, to which the reader responds in ways analogous to the customary marks of punctuation. Yet I am doubtful of the argument that would suggest that the reader, as his or her eye follows the poem from the right side of the page at the line end to the left side at the line beginning below, necessarily breaks or pauses significantly in the process of absorbing the written words. Prose, too, is written in lines, yet no one, so far as I know, is arguing that the eye-movements necessary in moving from line to line in prose occasion pauses analogous to the effect of punctuation. Few surely can have handed their prose manuscripts to compositors with clear indications of acceptable and unacceptable line divisions. But many aspects of how people read poetry await empirical investigation.

Dryden and others, however, may well be responding to contemporary expectations that lineation and syntax should generally correspond, though I am uncertain as to whether they would have developed the argument explicitly and whether the justification would have been couched in such quasi-psychological terms. Milton's own verse, even at its most free, often shows a correspondence between sentence and clause divisions and lineation, though he is certainly deviant from the statistical norms of his period. In an age which looked for syntax and lineation to correspond within quite narrowly circumscribed patterns, deviation can seem shocking and arresting. The first lines of the first poem in Donne's *Songs and Sonets* may well disconcert a modern reader, and must have struck his contemporaries as the bugle call of a new aesthetic:

> I wonder by my troth, what thou, and I
> Did, till we lov'd? were we not wean'd till then?
>   ('The good-morrow', lines 1–2)[16]

The terminal 'I' is startling, rendering the line partially palindromic, and enigmatic. Readers do not expect lines of poems to end with pronouns, at least pronouns functioning as subjects. The effect achieved is baroque, self-reflexive: by challenging the convention of syntax corresponding to lineation Donne pronounces it to be exactly that, convention, not nature, and perhaps lays open the conventionality, the arbitrariness, the artifice that underwrites all art, including 'The good-morrow'.

However, for reasons which relate to the scale and frequency of his practice, I am reluctant to interpret Milton's deviation in this way. I should estimate that something in the region of 5,000 of the 10,500 lines of *Paradise Lost* have line endings which intersect clausal divisions. Within the sample, the line division separates subject from verb or verb from object or copula from complement in 58.7 per cent of examples. Elsewhere the division is between such structures and phrases as prepositional phrases.

Although a similar or higher proportion of intraclausal line divisions separate subject, verb, object, etc., their overall frequency, especially in non-Miltonic texts, is very markedly lower. In *Paradise Lost* Milton seems to redefine the lineation conventions of English poetry and to re-educate his readers' expectations. He slackens the relationship, both at sentence and clausal level, between syntax and line division into looser, less persistent correlation.

I do not dispute that line divisions sometimes contribute to a neatly turned stylistic effect, almost a trick of style. Archie Burnett, for example, has written sensitively of passages in *Paradise Lost* where the line ending and the necessary backward and downward movement of the reader's eye are suggestive of the actions described within the poem, as in:

> Satan from hence now on the lower stair
> That scaled by steps of gold to heaven gate
> Looks down with wonder at the sudden view
> Of all this world at once.
>
> (III.540–3)

Here, Burnett observes, 'the reader "looks down" with Satan'.[17] Such effects, if we take them to be more than happy coincidence, seem an extraordinary achievement by a blind man, as Burnett notes. Yet intraclausal division is too pervasive for each example to command that sort of interpretative ingenuity. Quite simply, it is a normal way for a line of *Paradise Lost* to end. What critical inventiveness may be expended on such run-of-the-mill examples as:

> How hast thou instilled
> Thy malice into thousands, once upright
> And faithful, now proved false[?]
>
> (VI.269–71)

> The grassy clods now calved, now half appeared
> The tawny lion, pawing to get free
> His hinder parts, then springs as broke from bonds,
> And rampant shakes his brinded mane; the ounce,
> The libbard, and the tiger, as the mole

> Rising, the crumbled earth above them threw
> In hillocks; the swift stag from underground
> Bore up his branching head: scarce from his mould
> Behemoth biggest born of earth upheaved
> His vastness.
>
> (VII.463–72)

I wonder how anxious his readers should be that their downward eye-movement must in the first example follow '*up*right', while in the second example a long series of terms describing rising and lifting follows the line breaks. I doubt if readers re-educated by Milton to expect such divisions notice any discord.

The terms which Milton used in his note on the verse with which he prefaced the second edition of *Paradise Lost* may well be pertinent here.[18] His concerns were with his most obvious and controversial prosodic innovation, his use of 'verse without rhyme'. In a tone familiar from his polemics of the 1640s, he once more attacks the traditional retention of a barbarous custom. In the obligation to rhyme, his contemporaries, 'carried away by custom', have been constrained to adjust their natural expressive impulses to serve the exigencies of a convention which he regards as theoretically unsupported and unsupportable. I think Milton's attitude to lineation and syntax may well reflect the same impatience within gratuitous and conventional 'hindrance'. Milton produces a poetic texture in which those discourse markers which distinguish poetry and prose operate less frequently or not at all. Yet the status of *Paradise Lost* as an example of a poetic mode of discourse is unquestionable save in the rhetoric of the most vexatious of its opponents. But by removing the sorts of arbitrary constraint imposed on poetic syntax by the exigencies of lineation, Milton may develop sentence structures within a wider range of options, and may thus produce more easily the sentences of the kind of clausal complexity which we have been considering and which I have identified as a major distinguishing feature of his style. It is not that *Paradise Lost* gravitates towards some species of prose; rather, Milton, in producing a poetic texture capable of expressing a complexity of argument and subtlety of rhetoric analogous to that of his prose, eases off or abandons those conventional markers of poetic discourse which otherwise constrain syntactic options.

Milton's Minor Poems

As I have suggested, Milton's minor poetry differs markedly from the longer poems in terms of sentence structure and those aspects of prosody which relate to syntactic considerations. His practice approximates more closely to contemporary norms than to the Miltonic predilections which emerge elsewhere. Sentences in the minor poems are shorter and simpler not only than those of the rest of Milton but also than the averages among his contemporaries (table 2.18). Milton was writing his shorter poems from the age of fifteen ('A Paraphrase on Psalm cxiv') to the age of fifty or thereabouts (Sonnet XIX: 'Methought I saw my late espoused saint'). If we divide them into the early verse (that preceding 'Lycidas') and the poetry produced in 1637 and later, a pattern of increasing complexity emerges. Whereas the young Milton produces, by any criteria, sentences of shorter average length than his contemporaries, the sentences of the maturer Milton marginally exceed contemporary norms in terms of length in syllables

Table 2.18 Sentence length (with special reference to the minor poems)

	Number of words	Number of syllables	Number of clauses
Milton's minor poems	18.9	24.0	2.6
Minor poems before 'Lycidas'	16.6	22.0	2.2
Minor poems after 'Lycidas'	20.9	25.7	2.9
Milton's other poems	24.4	32.2	3.8
Non-Miltonic poems	18.5	22.9	2.9

and words, but still come closer to the practices of others than to the averages of his own longer poetry.

I am reluctant to interpret differences within Milton's minor poetry simply as a process of maturation. If we compare sentence length in *Comus* (for the most part dating from 1634) with that of his other long poems, we find the earlier poem has, on average, longer sentences. Many factors probably obtain in determining both the distinctions between the minor poems and the rest of the oeuvre and the distinctions which obtain between the minor poems themselves. The term 'minor poems' perhaps works to obscure their diversity, both of subgenre and prosodic organization. There are sonnets, poems in couplets, stanzaic forms, and other arrangements, most significantly in 'Lycidas', in which a variety of rhyme scheme operates, most probably under Italian influence,[19] and a high proportion of the minor poems are translations from the Hebrew of the Psalms. Milton offers pastoral elegy, political poems, love poems, odes, some of which have a distinctly narrative dimension, meditational verse, even fragments of an aristocratic entertainment. A network of situational expectations obtain, to be satisfied, modified or disdained, as on each occasion Milton sees fit. A satisfactory account of syntactic aspects of his shorter poems really awaits a rather different kind of study, one in which all the principal kinds of poetry of the period are appraised properly from the point of view of their linguistic, prosodic and other norms. Alastair Fowler has suggested routes forward in the analysis and chronicling of the genres and subgenres of the English literary tradition, but his study, perceptive and suggestive though it is, illuminates how little we really know about those discourse markers by which we distinguish kinds of writing, either in our own period or, through a process of scholarly reconstruction, in early periods.[20]

Yet certain generalizations about the syntax of Milton's shorter poems may still be entertained, though their chief force may be to define more strikingly what is distinctive about his longer works and, I suppose, pre-eminently about *Paradise Lost*.

The sentence structure of the minor poems far more closely resembles that of the non-Miltonic sample than his practice in the longer works. Very long sentences, however defined, are much

Table 2.19   Sentence length in the minor poems: clauses per sentence

Number of clauses per sentence	Milton				Non-Miltonic sample	
	Minor poems		Longer poems			
	Number of sentences	%	Number of sentences	%	Number of sentences	%
1–4	55	83.3	290	71.3	256	83.4
5 or more	11	16.7	117	28.7	51	16.6

Chi-square 16.18200 with 2 d.f.; significance 0.0003.

Table 2.20   Plurality of subordination in the minor poems

Number of subordinate clauses directly dependent on the main clause per sentence	Milton				Non-Miltonic sample	
	Minor poems		Longer poems			
	Number of sentences	%	Number of sentences	%	Number of sentences	%
0	34	51.5	124	30.5	124	40.5
1	18	27.3	145	35.6	98	31.9
2	6	9.1	73	17.9	51	16.6
3 or more	8	12.1	65	16.0	34	11.1

Chi-square 16.87435 with 6 d.f.; significance 0.0098.

rarer (table 2.19 shows the incidence of sentences of more than four clauses); multibranching of subordinate clauses around a main clause, which is in a minor way distinctive of Milton's poetry in general, is less a feature of the minor poems than of the control (table 2.20); and that predilection for lower subordination, for clauses dependent on other subordinate clauses, which is so quintessentially Miltonic, scarcely features (table 2.21). Poems as diverse in situation and aesthetic as 'L'Allegro' and the psalmic

Table 2.21 Lower subordination in the minor poems

| Number of clauses dependent on other subordinate clauses per sentence | Milton | | | | Non-Miltonic sample | |
| | Minor poems | | Longer poems | | | |
	Number of sentences	%	Number of sentences	%	Number of sentences	%
0	56	84.8	272	66.8	238	77.5
1	5	7.6	53	13.0	40	13.0
2	2	3.0	24	5.9	13	4.2
3 or more	3	4.5	58	14.3	16	5.2

Chi-square 23.76734 with 6 d.f.; significance 0.0006.

settings would seem, at least in these respects, to have more in common with each other – and with contemporary norms – than with Milton's longer poems, and arguments would seem to emerge for regarding them either as unexcitingly conformist or else as tactfully in step with prevailing literary decorums.

Burnett, whose intelligent and sensitive study of some aspects of Milton's style has, in passing, exposed the assumptions underpinning such arguments, cautions against them as 'little more than hastily indulged prejudices or crude abstractions'.[21] Again, whatever the orthodoxy of the sentence structure of such poems, other aspects may well prove more eccentric. Yet I think we may conclude that Milton challenges the syntactic restraints imposed by the verse forms less boldly here than elsewhere: his sentence structure, for the most part, closely resembles the usual practice of the times.

Though a general account such as this can only hint at it, especially in our present state of ignorance about the genre-specific aspects of style in seventeenth-century poetry, I suspect that the exigencies of insistent rhyme schemes may well have been a major factor in shaping practice. Whereas in Milton's longer poems, for the most part unrhymed, syntax and lineation are in a relatively loose relationship, in the minor poems a far higher proportion of sentences begin and/or end at a line division.

Table 2.22   Lineation and syntax in the minor poems

Type of sentence	Milton				Non-Miltonic sample	
	Minor poems		Longer poems			
	Number of sentences	%	Number of sentences	%	Number of sentences	%
both ends stopped	13	72.2	143	36.2	164	83.7
one end stopped	5	27.8	182	46.1	27	13.8
neither end stopped	0	–	70	17.7	5	2.6

Chi-square 123.49285 with 4 d.f.; significance 0.0000.

(Table 2.22 shows the pertinent information for sentences which begin and end in a pentameter line: analysis of tetrameter lines indicated a pronounced similarity between Milton's minor poems and contemporary norms, though sample size was small.) Especially in those poems which were either intended to be sung or else to simulate sung forms, such as the psalmic translations or the songs of 'Arcades', such a correspondence of line ending and syntactic division is appropriate and to be expected. The influence of rhyme scheme and of stanzaic division may quite clearly be discerned in a couple of aspects, though again, sample size is a little small. Milton, like his contemporaries, tends to contain sentences within couplets. Of the sentences in the sample which occur in poems written in couplets, we find only 21.4 per cent running on over a couplet division: in the non-Miltonic sample, the figure is 20.0 per cent. Stanzaic division is also inhibitive. In poems written in stanzas, 92.9 per cent of sentences do not run over from one stanza to the next: among contemporaries, the figure is 95.9 per cent, a statistically insignificant distinction. Prosodic decisions would seem to predetermine some of the syntactic choices open to poets, even ones as intrepidly innovative as Milton.

3

Lexis

Comus

The Elizabethan Milton?

'Monotony' and 'a certain sensuous poverty' are the terms in which F. R. Leavis usually characterizes Milton's style. But for some lines of *Comus* he avows an enthusiasm, lines where 'the momentary predominance in Milton of Shakespeare' produces a poetry which is 'richer, subtler and more sensitive' than in the other long poems of the oeuvre. Indeed, it is something of a critical commonplace that the texture of Milton's masque owes much to the influence of Elizabethan models, pre-eminently Shakespeare and Spenser.[1] That larger intertext no doubt repays critical attention, though it must rest outside the scope of this investigation. I shall, however, have something to say about Spenserian archaism and the lexis of *Comus*. Moreover, to call the style of *Comus* in some sense 'Elizabethan' begs the issue of what precisely does characterize the linguistic practice of Elizabethan poetry. There is much work to be done before we may respond with a well-founded confidence. Of Milton's masque, however, we may reasonably conclude that it is characterized by kinds of lexical inventiveness which contrast with some of his other writing and emerge starkly in juxtaposition with his other quasi-dramatic poem, *Samson Agonistes*.

Neologisms

Comus is less than 8,000 words long, yet I have noted almost sixty newly coined words, and probably I have missed some. In contrast, though *Samson Agonistes* is about 5,000 words longer, I have found there are only about a score of words apparently of Miltonic invention.[2]

Milton seems to have coined only the word 'haemony' (line 637) directly from a foreign language rather than from the native resources of English. This singularly opaque term for the magic herb which protects the Attendant Spirit and the Brothers from Comus's powers has offered a challenge to Miltonists as irresistible as the two-handed engine of 'Lycidas'. Milton elsewhere defends with some vehemence the practice of naturalizing foreign proper names into more English-seeming forms. He approves the Smectymnuans' practice 'in dealing with an outlandish name' of deleting 'a harsh forreigne termination' while retaining 'the radicall word'.[3] In the case of 'haemony', however, Milton in stripping the inflexion has produced a name which relates ambiguously and riddlingly to possible classical roots. Is it to be associated with 'Haemonia', a poetical name for Thessaly, a land associated with magic? Or with various alternative Greek words, 'haimonios' ('blood-red'); or 'haimon' ('skilful' or 'bloody'); or 'haema-oinos', the eucharistic blood–wine? Or 'hymen', the virginal membrane? Or the Hebrew 'aman' ('to believe')?[4] Yet the enigma serves well the decorum of the passage in which it appears, and probably could not have been achieved other than through the adoption of a foreign loan-word of such opacity. Milton produces in the Attendant Spirit's account of the herb a passage the level of seriousness of which defies final resolution. The Spirit has received haemony from 'a certain shepherd lad / Of small regard to see to' (lines 618–19). The unspecificity and openness of the text offers several interpretative strategies. Those who see here a sort of intimate personal allusion look to identify a reference to Charles Diodati or some other contemporary. Alternatively, the lines have been taken as a reference to Milton himself, and as an allusion to his sense of his own worth and present obscurity. Or else, if the lad is Milton, perhaps haemony, his gift, represents the power of poetry. An allegorical or theological reading interprets the shepherd to be a Christian figure, perhaps Paul, and gives to haemony a spiritual significance.[5] Milton, of course, could have closed down the alternatives, but chose not to, and the obscure naming of the gift suits well the enigma of its giver.

Other Miltonic neologisms within the poem are formed from the current resources of English by means of the usual processes of affixation or compounding. Some are fairly unremarkable, though they reflect perhaps an impulse towards poetic brevity or ellipsis. Hence, Comus speaks of 'near-ushering guides' (line 278), that is, guides that usher or escort from close by. The Severn stays Sabrina's flight 'with his cross-flowing course' (line 831). Sabrina heals 'with precious vialed liquors' (line 846), liquors contained in vials, with perhaps a secondary meaning of liquors kept in precious vials. Comus has Nature retain 'the all-worshipped ore' (line 718). His rout cannot 'perceive their foul disfigurement' (line 74), that which disfigures them.

However, the coinings often have at least a little more of interest than mere brevity. Thus, the 'knot-grass' on which the Attendant Spirit's sheep are said to have grazed is 'dew-besprent' (line 541): '-besprent' is possibly an archaism and certainly a word Spenser uses.[6] Similarly, Milton coins 'azurn' in 'the azurn sheen / Of turkis blue' (lines 892–3) and 'cedarn' in 'about the cedarn alleys' (line 989), though 'azure' was current as an adjective and 'cedar' as an attributive. Carey is probably right that such words, with their perhaps rather antique suffix '-en', have something of the Spenserian flavour. Consider again:

> Two such I saw, what time the laboured ox
> In his loose traces from the furrow came,
> And the swinked hedger at his supper sat.
>
> (lines 290–2)

Milton forms 'swinked' ('wearied with toil', as the *OED* glosses) on close analogy with the unusual form 'laboured ox' ('oppressed with labour' – *OED* – a Shakespearian usage). It sounds surprising and a little puzzling: at first, I suppose, we try to read it as 'the hedger that has been swinked' rather than 'the hedger that has swinked too hard', until we reconstruct the meaning on the model of 'the laboured ox'. Yet it sounds authentically pastoral, deeply and anciently English, no doubt because 'swink' had probably

already assumed an archaic flavour. It is a term Spenser used,
though it had not been much current since Chaucer's day.[7]

Adjectival compounds accrete around personifications and allegorical or semi-allegorical figures within the poem. Neptune
assigns 'this isle' to his 'blue-haired deities' (lines 27, 29). Again
in:

> the grey-hooded Even
> Like a sad-votarist in palmer's weed
> Rose from the hind most wheels of Phoebus' wain
> (lines 187–9)

'grey-hooded', while precisely and sensitively suggestive of the
colours of twilight, ties in with the simile of the palmer and
initiates the process of personification realized within the passage. We variously encounter 'pure-eyed Faith' (line 212), 'that
snaky-headed Gorgon shield' (line 446), 'Thetis' tinsel-slippered
feet' (line 876) and Sabrina's 'coral-paven bed' (line 885). Such
adjectival compounds recur so frequently in such contexts that
they function within the poem almost as a stylistic motif.

Yet adjectival compounds are sometimes far from straightforward. Leavis has commented admirably on the lines:

> And set to work millions of spinning worms,
> That in their green shops weave the smooth-haired silk.
> (lines 714–15)

Leavis observes that 'smooth-haired', which is a Miltonic coining,
'plays off against the energy of the verse the tactual luxury of
stroking human hair or the living coat of an animal'.[8] Certainly it
disconcerts the reader a little, much as the metaphoric suggestion
of worms keeping shops does.[9] 'Hair' and 'hairy' would not seem
contemporaneously to have been used for cloth or clothing save
in the highly specific case of cloth made from hair. Assumptions
and preconceptions are nudged in these lines, as worms behave as
people and cloth has some of the attributes of a living thing.
Burnett sensitively remarks of 'the rushy-fringed bank' (line 889)
that 'rushy fringed', another of these compound neologisms,
'announces the orderliness of nature: the fringe may be the

ordinary edge of the river, but also an ornamental border', and as such, it carries considerable thematic weight, marking the true qualities of a benign nature in contrast with the spurious riot of Comus's version.[10]

Sometimes the compound adjectives carry quite complex allusions. Thus, among the dwellers of the 'broad fields of the sky', we encounter 'The Graces, and the rosy-bosomed Hours' (lines 978, 985). Why 'rosy-bosomed', we may wonder, until we recall that other attribute of the Hours in classical mythology, one invoked by Milton in 'In Obitum Praesulis Eliensis', that 'the fleeting Hours . . . rouse the day' (lines 39–40, Campbell's translation). The Hours in *Comus* appear appropriately suffused with the colour of the dawn.[11] Similarly, when Comus threatens the Lady:

> if I but wave this wand,
> Your nerves are all chained up in alabaster,
> And you a statue, or as Daphne was
> Root-bound, that fled Apollo
>
> (lines 658–61)

a substantial passage of Ovidian metamorphosis is suggested in that single word, 'root-bound', which perhaps also serves a secondary purpose, that of hinting at the limitations of Comus's powers. His threatened transformation would make her more rooted in her resolve (a current signification of 'rooted') and physically beyond the consummation of his seduction.[12] Again, the resonant phrase, 'the sun-clad power of chastity' (line 781), surely invokes recollection of Revelation 12:1, 'And there appeared a great wonder in heaven; a woman clothed with the sun . . .', which was traditionally interpreted, appropriately for the *Comus* context, as a Marian allusion.[13]

New Senses

New senses are harder for a modern reader to pick up than new words, especially in a poem so well known and so widely influential as *Comus*. What was fresh and striking may well have been rendered trite and commonplace by familiarity: 'tripping the light fantastic' (from 'L'Allegro', lines 33–4) has lost much of its charm.

Nevertheless, I have found just under thirty examples of words which Milton would seem to have pushed or stretched from contemporaneously current significations. Generally, they are nouns which Milton uses attributively in innovative ways or adjectives which Milton uses either of abstractions (where previously they had related to concrete things) or in other ways which stretch their familiar role.

Thus, Milton extends the semantic range of 'tipsy' in 'Tipsy dance' (line 104) from meaning, to quote the *OED*, 'Affected with liquor so as to be unable to walk or stand steadily', to 'Characterized or accompanied by intoxication'. The phrase has perhaps a slight oxymoronic force: the revellers are too drunk to stand but they can dance, after a fashion. Consider the force of the attributive 'tap'stry' in:

> honest-offered courtesy,
> Which oft is sooner found in lowly sheds
> With smoky rafters, than in tap'stry halls
> And courts of princes.
>
> (lines 321–4)

Earlier the word when used attributively had a narrow signification, as in 'tapestry hanging' or 'tapestry clothes'. Here it implies something larger than merely halls for hanging tapestries; it functions as a social and cultural signifier, the sort of hall where tapestries are hung. It connotes affluence and perhaps excess in a rather vaguer way, much as nowadays the attributive in the phrase 'champagne socialist' operates rather differently from how it functions in the phrase 'champagne glass' or 'champagne cork'. Again, the force of 'urchin' in 'all urchin blasts, and ill-luck signs / That the . . . elf delights to make' (lines 844–5) seems more complex than earlier attributive uses, suggesting at once something of the mischief-making of the elf (*OED* 1.c), the keen prickliness of the hedgehog (*OED* 1.a), and perhaps even the wanton destructiveness of the roguish youngster (*OED* 4).[14]

Milton's extension of adjectives customarily used of concrete nouns to abstracts could alternatively be considered as an aspect of collocational abnormality or sometimes in more traditional terms as a concomitant of personification. Thus, we find 'gladly banish squint suspicion' (line 412), whereas 'squint' was customarily used of eyes or a human expression. Others had used 'banish' to mean expel a thing or an abstract notion, but perhaps in this phrase we recall first its primary signification of rejecting a person. The line nudges us towards recognizing a partially formed personification. Again, the Lady's charge that Comus has 'betrayed my credulous innocence / With vizored falsehood' (lines 696–7) is lexically interesting, in that 'credulous' formerly referred only to people and not to abstractions, and, probably more significantly, so too, it would seem, did 'vizored'. Falsehood appears briefly like a figure from Spenserian allegory, but the mode is not maintained.

Unusual Collocations

In an interesting cluster of examples Milton pushes the signification of words customarily referent to more substantial or tactile phenomena to apply to the air or to the heavens. Editors, no doubt correctly, have noted in the phrase 'The pillared firmament' (line 597) an allusion to Job 26:11, 'The pillars of heaven tremble'. It is, however, the first occasion noted by the *OED* in which the participial adjectives qualifies something as remote and non-tactile as the heavens. As Comus describes the teeming fertility of nature he speaks of 'the winged air darked with plumes' (line 729). 'Air' does not usually collocate with colour words, and 'winged' is here used in what the *OED* regards as a new signification, 'Full of wings; crowded with wings' (1.c). Previously only flying creatures or, poetically, boats were spoken of as 'winged'. Again, the Attendant Spirit sings as Sabrina descends:

> Summer drouth, or singed air
> Never scorch thy tresses fair
> (lines 927–8)

The *OED* records no context in which 'singe', either as verb or noun or participial adjective, collocates with something as immaterial as air. Hair or surfaces are singed: air has no surfaces, yet Milton makes it seem more of a physical presence than it usually appears. The Attendant Spirit prepares to leave for 'the green earth's end, / Where the bowed welkin slow doth bend' (lines 1013–14). Conceptually, Milton's – and our own – cosmology would require the sky to be curved around the world, yet neither he nor we could perceive it as such, nor, it would seem, was the word 'bowed' used of the immaterial, but rather of branches and staves. Comus tells the Lady about seeing her brothers:

> I took it for a faery vision
> Of some gay creatures of the element
> That in the colours of the rainbow live
> And play i' the plighted clouds
> (lines 297–300)

'The element', as editors have noted, means simply 'the sky' (*OED* 10.a). But how may creatures live *in* the colours of the rainbow? Comus indicates that in fairy fashion colours – and here the colours of that most insubstantial phenomenon, the rainbow – have a substantiality for such creatures which they do not have for mortals. 'Plighted', which Carey glosses as 'folded', a cognate of 'pleated', customarily qualified clothing or hair. Milton uses the word himself in the *History of England*: 'she [Boadicea] wore a plighted Garment of divers colours' (*CPW*, V.81).[15] Milton's abnormal collocation suggests that clouds have the tactility of garments. Similarly, 'liquid' had collocated in poetic discourse with 'air' as signifier for clarity and transparency at least since Spenser (*OED* 2), but Milton joltingly revivifies the commonplace in the Attendant Spirit's 'There I *suck* the liquid air' (line 979, my italics).[16]

If *Comus* is indeed to be perceived as Milton's most Shakespearian poem, I suppose the analogue which most strongly suggests itself is *The Tempest*, with its masque, the central figure of the magician, and its gestures towards pastoral and the fairy world. Yet comparison points up neatly an area of sharp contrast in sensibility. For Shakespeare in his last phrase, dissolving cloud and thin air are fit symbols for the impermanence and ultimate insubstantiality of all secular experience:

> These our actors,
> As I foretold you, were all spirits, and
> Are melted into air, into thin air:
> And, like the baseless fabric of this vision,
> The cloud-capp'd towers, the gorgeous palaces,
> The solemn temples, the great globe itself,
> Yea, all which it inherit, shall dissolve,
> And, like this insubstantial pageant faded,
> Leave not a rack behind.[17]

Quite conversely, air and cloud for Milton do not emblematize insubstantiality. Rather, his poetic imagination, feeding off an intellectual awareness of the actual materiality of entities which the senses may suggest are immaterial, produces an image of the universe that attributes body, weight and presence to air and cloud and sky.

Samson Agonistes

Neologisms

Not only are words of Miltonic coining much rarer in *Samson Agonistes* than in *Comus*, but also for the most part they contribute little liveliness to the style. Some are simple compounds yoking attributives to the nouns they qualify: 'sea-idol' (line 13), 'Love-quarrels' (line 1008) and 'wedlock-treachery' (line 1009). 'Tongue-batteries' is produced to fit the context of an extended image in which Dalila's attempt on Samson is seen as a military assault:

> With blandished parleys, feminine assaults,
> Tongue-batteries, she surceased not day nor night
> To storm me over-watched, and wearied out.
> (lines 403–5)

The word itself, out of context, appears quite exciting, an unusual juxtaposition of the small ('tongue') and the powerful ('batteries'). In context, however, it serves merely to make the connections of vehicle and tenor even more obvious. *Samson Agonistes* is a text which, at the level of texture, rarely baffles or excites.

I noted earlier the high incidence within *Samson Agonistes* of words containing or cognate with the element 'self', which relate to the thematic structure of the poem. A number of these are coined by Milton to foreground issues of selfhood among the Hebrews; 'self-satisfying' (line 306), 'self-rigorous' (line 513), 'self-displeased' (line 514) and 'self-severe' (line 827).[18] The neologism 'unforeskinned' in Harapha's sneer, 'Palestine, won by a Philistine / From the unforeskinned race' (lines 1099–100), is similarly a specifically Philistian comment: obviously it demeans a people to categorize them according to the presence or absence of their prepuces.[19]

Coinings directly from classical tongues are very few. Milton produces 'Chalybean-tempered steel' (line 133) from the 'Chalybes', the name of an ancient nation of Asia Minor famed in classical writings for their metalworking. More puzzling, perhaps, is his coining, it would seem from late Latin, of 'obstriction' (line 312), seemingly to mean 'obligation'. The words 'obstrict' and 'obstrictive' had been used earlier, but very rarely. The late Latin *obstrictio* seems to have been current in legal documents:[20] what Milton sought to connote by adopting it remains open to interpretation. Something, perhaps, of the dark legalism of Judaism from which Christianity liberates its believers. Certainly, in his prose, Milton persistently repudiated the application of Old Testament legal niceties to the Christian era, a process which he terms 'sow[ing] up that Jewish vail which Christ by his death on the Crosse rent in sunder'. Again, of practices founded on Jewish ecclesiastical law, he says, 'that which to the Jew but jewish is to the Christian no better than Canaanitish' (*Reason of Church-Government*, *CPW*, I.839, 845). To associate Jewish legalism with the rebarbative terminology of diplomatic Latin may well have had an expressive force.[21]

New Senses

On scarcely more than a dozen occasions in *Samson Agonistes* Milton effects a semantic shift in words already current in English. They generally show at least a touch of lexical delicacy. Thus, when the Chorus speak of 'An amber scent of odorous perfume' (line 720), Milton is extending the adjective, which had previously alluded to the colour of amber, in allusion to the fragrance of burnt amber or of the oil of amber. Yet it suggests, too, the intensity of the fragrance, so powerful it seems almost visible. Milton makes of one of God's attributes, the fact that he is without boundary in space and time, a new synonym, 'the interminable' (line 307), through the absolute extension of a current adjective. 'Separate' in 'a person [meaning Samson] separate to God' (line 31) possibly anticipates the *OED*'s first record of sense 2.b, 'Belonging or peculiar to one'. Carey notes that the word invokes recollection of the Hebrew, in that 'Nazarite', which defines Samson's status, is derived from the Hebrew word meaning 'to separate oneself'.[22]

One neat synecdochic extension produces a slight, uttered by the Chorus, which matches Harapha's sneer at the 'unforeskinned race':[23]

> Then with what trivial weapon came to hand,
> The jaw of a dead ass, his sword of bone,
> A thousand foreskins fell, the flower of Palestine.
>   (lines 142–4)

The *OED* does not note the incidence of 'foreskin' to mean, as here it must, 'uncircumsized person'. The term seems demeaning, much as Harapha's does, in that people are reduced to this most exiguous token of their Jewish or Gentile status. In this context, however, a lexical playfulness obtains. The thousand foreskins fall through the agency of the 'sword of bone': Samson appears as grotesque circumcizer of the Philistian people.

Paradise Regained

Neologisms

Neologizing in *Paradise Regained* is on the same reduced scale as in *Samson Agonistes*, and the expressive value of coinings is similarly muted. Once more, compound adjectives predominate, such as 'long-threatened' (I.59), 'rich-clad' (II.352) and 'self-deceived' (IV.7).

Some seem a little more evocative. The 'beasts of chase, or fowl of game' are proffered to Christ 'boiled, / Grisamber-steamed' (II.343–4), presumably steamed over a fire made fragrant with ambergris, which suggests a cuisine both extravagant and contrived. 'Thick-warbled' in 'the Attic bird / Trills her thick-warbled notes the summer long' (IV.245–6) puzzles a little. Editors usually recognize an allusion to the nightingale, but the component 'thick-' could suggest either the density and frequence of its song (*OED* 2 and 3) or else that the song is confusedly articulated (*OED* 4). Other coinings include the formation through prefixing of 'unconniving' (I.363) and 'unpredict', a perhaps surprising negation of a verb one may not have expected to be tractable to such affixation:

> Means I must use thou say'st, prediction else
> Will unpredict and fail me of the throne.
> (III.394–5)

Christ's quibbling phrase occurs as part of his reductive restatement of Satan's argument, and the problematic formula (in what senses can 'prediction . . . unpredict'?) discloses the internal incoherence of his adversary's case. A prediction revoked loses its status *qua* prediction. The unpredicting prediction discloses Satanic duncery. Satan's term 'over-sure' in his caveat to the fallen angels supports a similar point:

> Therefore I am returned, lest confidence
> Of my success with Eve in Paradise
> Deceive ye to persuasion over-sure
> Of like succeeding here.
> (II.140–3)

A 'sure' or certain persuasion is one presumably based on the weight and conviction carried by a presentation of the evidence. A persuasion which is 'over-sure', that is, more sure than the evidence supports, is more correctly not sure at all: the word does not naturally admit of the intensifying prefix.

New Senses

Semantic extensions in *Paradise Regained* are fairly infrequent (I note less than a score) but show a neat lexical control. Several in various ways point towards the concretization of abstractions. In ways which the *OED* has not noted, Milton uses a couple of words attributively, seemingly for the first time. Thus he writes, 'conqueror Death discover[s] them scarce men' (III.85), and 'Let his tormentor conscience find him out' (IV.130). Both 'conqueror' and 'tormentor' were customarily used of human agents and their adoption in these contexts contributes to a muted sort of personification.

In other ways terms for large abstractions are nudged towards concreteness. 'Gluttony', the deadly sin, is reapplied to mean an example of that sin, perhaps on analogy with the current semantic extension of 'lechery', in Christ's dismissal, in a phrase that would not have been out of place in *Of Reformation*, of 'Their sumptuous gluttonies, and gorgeous feasts' (IV.114). God the Father speaks of Satan's boasts 'to the throng / Of his apostasy' (I.145–6), an extension of the abstract which the *OED* has not noted, though editors have. MacKellar judiciously observes of these lines that 'Milton's abstract terms are often more suggestive and hence more poetic than the corresponding concrete terms'.[24] But what would indeed be the corresponding term for Milton's resonant phrase? 'The throng of his apostasy' implies at once 'his fellow-apostates' and 'the throng produced by his apostasy'. Again, Satan disappears 'bowing low / His grey dissimulation' (I.497–8): the *OED* notes this example as the first use of 'dissimulation' as a concrete manifestation of the process of dissimulation, a dissimulated or disguised form. Primarily the lines mean that he bows the grey head he has assumed as part of role of 'an aged man in rural weeds' (I.314). But 'grey dissimulation' perhaps connotes something of the greyness or indistinctiveness of dissimulation.

I noted with particular reference to *Comus* a Miltonic habit of depicting through subtle lexical adjustments atmospheric and cosmic phenomena in an unusually concrete way. Thus, the 'pillared firmament' of *Comus* (line 597) returns as 'the pillared frame of heaven (*PR*, IV.455). Again, in a teasing phrase Satan speaks of 'all the quartered winds' (IV.202). The *OED* identifies a new signification here for 'quartered', which it glosses no doubt correctly as 'Belonging to a quarter or part of the horizon'. Yet 'quartered' in the mid-seventeenth century most frequently meant lodged in quarters, often in a military sense. The winds, I feel, not only belong to part of the horizon, but also in some secondary way seem physically to be stored there until they blow. We recognize, perhaps, a submerged allusion to the Cave of Aeolus (*Aeneid*, I.52–5, *Odyssey*, X.2ff.).

A passage of extraordinary power, describing the storm to which Satan subjects Christ, works in part through such mechanisms:

> either tropic now
> 'Gan thunder, and both ends of heaven, the clouds
> From many a horrid rift abortive poured
> Fierce rain with lightning mixed, water with fire
> In ruin reconciled: nor slept the winds
> Within their stony caves, but rushed abroad
> From the four hinges of the world, and fell
> On the vexed wilderness.
>
> (IV.409–16)

Carey notes that the *OED* instances no sense of the word 'tropic' that would be appropriate here, though perhaps he concludes prematurely that Milton is using it loosely.[25] I think that we have here a conceptual riot to match the riot of the universe. Plainly we are to note some distinction between 'either tropic' and 'both ends of heaven', but 'tropics' and 'ends' invoke radically different ways of perceiving. The customary meaning of 'tropic' is one of the two lines of latitude which correspond to the solsticial points at which the sun reaches its furthest range north or south of the Equator. Milton is extending the word a little, shifting it from an abstract astronomic concept into regions corresponding to that concept, those parts of the earth's surface which correspond to the Tropics of Cancer and Capricorn. Those areas are necessarily hoop-shaped, ringing the earth. Moreover, since the Holy Land is to the north of the northern tropic, Christ could not have distinguished them: thunder from either tropic would have been perceived by him as thunder from the southern horizon. The poet, as it were, here stands outside the perception of the hero, viewing the universal storm as if from a point remote from the earth. Yet, though tropics are circles, the two 'ends of heaven' must be the terminations of an entity that has length and some width, the diametrically opposed sections at which Christ perceives the heavens to meet the horizon. Viewed from the position at which one can perceive the tropics – or viewed from the position of astronomical theory – the earth has no ends: 'both ends of heaven' implies a limited, anthropocentric, ground-level way of seeing the world. The 'four hinges of the world' may indeed mean no more than the four cardinal points of the compass, such as Christ may have perceived them, on the ground in a particular location, or else they too may invoke an alternative, and in this case fancifully poetic, notion about the nature and disposition of the universe. 'Water with fire / In ruin reconciled' finds fit parallel in the sorts of intellectual reconciliation Milton expects of his readers.

Unusual Collocations

Again *Paradise Regained* discloses a few interesting innovations, usually in the direction of concretization: words normally collocating with concrete or animate nouns collocate instead with more insubstantial entities. Thus Christ muses, 'O what a multitude of thoughts at once / Awakened in me swarm' (1.196–7): 'swarm' is a verb usually used of animate creatures, often non-human ones, and 'awakened', too, is used usually of things that can be said to sleep. In a sub-metaphoric way, Milton associates Christ's mental agitation with the disturbances of a stimulated hive. Again, in the sense which is relevant, 'compose' usually collocates with material objects – someone or something is composed of some material substance: Christ denounces that archetypal fraudster as one who is composed of the immaterial – he is 'composed of lies' (1.407).

Other unusual and interesting collocations fall outside the principal group. For example, 'couple', meaning 'to copulate', seems mainly to refer to the activities of animals rather than humans: when Satan speaks of Belial and his 'lusty crew' who 'Cast wanton eyes on the daughters of men, / And coupled with them' (II.178, 180–1), the miscegenation has a bestial tinge.

Ludic Lexis in *Paradise Regained*, *Samson Agonistes* and *Comus*

All the Miltonic poems we have considered so far show, at least at some points, elements of lexical playfulness. We find word-play in the narrowest sense, plays or puns upon the alternative significance of words or even at times, though usually in muted fashion, plays on homonymic ambiguity. The ludic element extends to quibbles and neat distinctions about alternative meanings of words and to some of the more interesting of the neologisms, semantic shifts and extensions, and the collocational abnormalities already discussed. Certain essentially lexical figures such as oxymoron and zeugma possess a ludic quality both specifically in Milton and probably more generally. However, like humour itself, the playful, protean stuff defies definition and therefore objective quantification, though not comment. Moreover, Milton can be as grimly playful as his God can be grimly humorous. Le Comte has admirably reminded us both of the potential seriousness of punning and of the subjectivity inherent in identifying puns.[26]

I consider a sportive use of language to be quite an important element in *Comus* and *Samson Agonistes*, but it is much more powerfully present in *Paradise Regained*, both the tone and texture of which have been rather undervalued by critical orthodoxy.[27]

The juxtaposition of cognate words produces a sort of dense, quibbling effect on occasions. Thus the sybaritic Comus offers the maxim that 'It is for homely features to keep home' (line 747). 'Homely', through a long process of semantic shift, had already arrived at its modern signification of plain or uncomely. The line revitalizes our sense of its original meaning and offers a kind of oblique etymology: Comus adds, 'They had their name thence' (line 748). Consider the not dissimilar words of Manoa to Samson:

[The Philistines] proclaim
Great pomp, and sacrifice, and praises loud
To Dagon, as their god who hath delivered
Thee Samson bound and blind into their hands,
Them out of thine, who slew'st them many a slain.

                                              (lines 435–9)

Samson, of course, slew the living, not the slain. The latter term
functions proleptically. It anticipates their status once Samson
has finished with them. In a sense, as he encounters them they are
as good as dead. The neatly turned distinction between 'their
god . . . hath delivered thee into their hands' and '[their god hath
delivered] Them out of thine' rests on two meanings of 'deliver',
first, 'to hand over to another's possession' (*OED* 6), and, second, 'to set free, liberate' (*OED* 1).

Both poems have an interesting play on 'liquid', which in
seventeenth-century English had not only its modern meaning
but also, in poetry, a meaning analogous to the Latin *liquidus*,
'clear, transparent, bright'. The chorus speaks of Samson,
'Whose drink was only from the liquid brook' (line 557). The
lexical environment of 'drink' and 'brook' pushes the reader
towards the former signification, which confronts us, however,
with an apparent pleonasm: of course the brook is liquid –
Samson drank it. The momentary puzzle resolves itself when we
recall instead the poetic usage of the word. Unsurprisingly,
'liquid' (=*liquidus*) collocates more usually with words for air,
light and fire. Milton's use as modifier of 'brook' challenges
comprehension. We have noted earlier (see p. 57) the revived
impact of 'liquid air', sucked by the Attendant Spirit (lines
975–9).

Juxtaposition of cognate words and the quibbling repetition of
the same word in different senses catches the attention throughout *Paradise Regained*. In what Raleigh terms Milton's 'worst
pun'[28] Milton has Christ dream he stood by the brook of Cherith

And saw the ravens with their horny beaks
Food to Elijah bringing even and morn,
Though ravenous, taught to abstain from what they brought.

                                              (II.267–9)

I doubt whether the pun is quite so atrocious as editors pretend, nor need we invoke changes in literary aesthetic to defend it.[29] Milton is defining the points of similarity and distinction between, on the one hand, Christ, and, on the other, both Elijah and the lower creatures. Since Elijah ate of the bread, it must be that Christ in his dream declines to eat of the food: he, not Elijah, has been 'taught to abstain'. Thus Christ shares with the ravens (and by implication with Elijah) the characteristic of feeling hunger, but transcends them by his election to abstain. If Milton thought 'raven' and 'ravenous' to be etymologically cognate, then he erred – the one is from Old English, the other from Old French – but it was an error that persisted in English lexicography at least into Dr Johnson's *Dictionary*. Other examples seem no more (nor less) than neat turns of phrase. Thus, Satan's malice prompts him 'cruelly to afflict [Job] / With all inflictions' (I.425–6).

The more playful aspects of language cluster around those parts of the text in which Milton is considering Christ's resistance to the allurements of the political and cultural establishment. The richest passage describes Satan's vision of military prowess:

> [Christ] looked and saw what numbers numberless
> The city gates outpoured, light-armed troops
> In coats of mail and military pride;
> In mail their horses clad, yet fleet and strong,
> Prancing their riders bore, the flower and choice
> Of many provinces from bound to bound;
>
> .   .   .   .
>
> He saw them in their forms of battled ranged,
> How quick they wheeled, and flying behind them shot
> Sharp sleet of arrowy showers against the face
> Of their pursuers, and overcame by flight;
> The field all iron cast a gleaming brown,
> Nor wanted clouds of foot, nor on each horn,
> Cuirassiers all in steel for standing fight;
> Chariots and elephants endorsed with towers
> Of archers, nor of labouring pioneers
> A multitude with spades and axes armed
> To lay hills plain, fell woods, or valleys fill,
> Or where plain was raise hill, or overlay
> With bridges rivers proud, as with a yoke.
>
> (III.310–34)

The seeming nonsense of 'numbers numberless' flags the quasi-satirical tone. There follows the reductive syllepsis of 'In coats of mail and military pride', in which the pride appears equated with some garment assumed for the nonce. Note the syntactic ambiguity of 'from bound to bound', which could relate either to the provinces from which the riders come or to the eccentric 'prancing' of the horses, carrying the riders from prancing stride to prancing stride in the unnatural equitation perfected by renaissance equestrians. 'Shower' was the normal word for a flight of arrows, but Milton partially revives the metaphor in 'Sharp sleet of arrowy showers' – but can one have a 'sleet of showers', rather than a 'shower of sleet'? And surely sleet is soft, not sharp. The image seems significantly inept. Again, the meaning of 'The field all iron cast a gleaming brown' is awkward to define. Presumably the field is the subject and 'all iron' is in parenthesis to it: 'cast' suggests the spreading of a hue, the 'gleaming brown'. But the collocation of 'cast' and 'iron' perhaps hints at another structure in which the iron casts or fashions metallurgically the field into a brown object. 'Gleaming brown' seems an odd collocate, as if one should say 'bright grey', till we recall that 'brown' could mean 'burnished'. 'Clouds', meaning a large group of people, is a semantic extension familiar in seventeenth-century English from the biblical phrase 'a cloud of witnesses' (Hebrews 12:1) and no doubt, as editors usually note, there is an echo, too, of Virgil's 'nimbus peditum' (*Aeneid*, VII.793). Yet surely the phrase, with the awkward though familiar synecdoche, has in English some of the oddness of mixed metaphor: 'clouds of foot' at least suggests the infelicity of 'clouds of feet'. Then the reader must negotiate the elephantine pun on 'endorsed', which as Carey notes has both the sense 'carrying on their backs' and the sense 'confirmed, strengthened', a piece of word-play which undermines the seriousness of the description. The passage may seem redeemed by the grandiloquent account of the pioneer corps levelling hills and filling valleys till the reader recognizes this seeming glory as a vainglorious version of the favourite army exercise of digging holes to fill them in again. Throughout the passage Milton's unstable use of language, our uncertainty about seriousness and meaning, the barely suppressed absurdity of expression together subvert the vision, preparing the reader for Christ's response, his 'unmoved' rejection of 'Much ostentation vain of fleshly arm, / And fragile arms' (III.387–8), itself a contemptuous quibble.

Others have noted how a judicious selection of terminology ties those forces Christ opposes to the apparatuses of the seventeenth-century church and state. Thus in dismay the fallen angels resolve to invest all power in Satan:

> Unanimous they all commit the care
> And management of this main enterprise
> To him their great dictator.
>
> (I.111–13)

The term had a certain currency in mid-century political theory as the appropriate nomenclature for a leader sought in dire circumstances and for a restricted period.[30] Milton may perhaps be alluding to episodes of English history, such as the appointment of Cromwell as Lord Protector and the temporary assumption of power by General Monck, both of which proved malign to republican aspirations. Again:

> [Satan] To council summons all his mighty peers,
> Within thick clouds and dark tenfold involved,
> A gloomy consistory.
>
> (I.40–2)

Carey sees here an ironic reference to the ecclesiastical senate in which the Pope presides over the body of cardinals and to the bishop's court for ecclesiastical cases in the Anglican church.[31] The latter usage, I feel, may be more pertinent. Certainly, as I have lately concluded, much in *Paradise Regained* reasserts obliquely the republican and puritan values of its author,[32] and such neat linguistic cross-tagging playfully restates the connections.

The Minor Poems

Milton's minor poems include exercises in a very wide range of genre (hymns, translations, satirical verse, aristocratic entertainment, pastoral elegy, poems of compliment and others) composed from adolescence to mature middle age. Generalization presents difficulties, not only because of the diversity but because some are brief and several, such as the translations which grace the title-pages of prose works, are decidedly slight. Poems which antedate the Civil War seem lexically akin to *Comus*, whereas I find relatively little innovation or eccentricity in the lexis of later work.

Neologisms

Words seemingly of Miltonic formation occur very frequently in the early poetry, and I note some examples from later poems. Some reflect no more than his familiar impatience with the available current word-stock, an impatience manifest in the coining of words using the established resources of the language. Thus, from 'mute' he coins 'mutely' in 'Driving dumb silence from the portal door, / Where he had mutely sat two years before' ('At a Vacation Exercise', lines 5–6). 'Timelessly', another adverb generated through the usual process of affixation, may momentarily puzzle when we encounter it in the opening lines of 'On the Death of a Fair Infant':

> O fairest flower no sooner blown but blasted,
> Soft silken primrose fading timelessly.
> (lines 1–2)

How may a process of mutability occur 'timelessly' or out of time, we may ponder. However, 'timeless' contemporaneously meant merely 'out of due time' – the other sense is first recorded from a text a little later than Milton's. In the same poem, 'sheeny' in 'did of late Earth's sons besiege the wall / Of sheeny heaven' ('On the Death of a Fair Infant', lines 47–8) sounds stronger, perhaps, than 'shiny', indicative of a more vibrant brilliance. Milton in his early writing rather liked the word 'sheen' – he uses it of turquoise, of stars, of heaven and of saints' raiments (*Comus*, lines 892, 1002; Nativity Ode, line 145; 'Epitaph on the Marchioness of Winchester', line 73), and the adjective constituted a useful addition to the vocabulary of English literature, and particularly poetic discourse. The *OED* records examples from Pope's assistant, Elijah Fenton, himself an editor of Milton, from Collins, Tennyson and Matthew Arnold – it was evidently a useful word once, if now perhaps fallen into desuetude. Again, 'saintly' in 'saintly shout, and solemn jubilee' ('At a Solemn Music', line 9) antedates by almost thirty years the first *OED* record of the adjectival use of the term. It balances neatly the two-syllabled adjective, 'solemn', which qualifies the parallel word and with which it alliterates. 'Stall-reader' in 'Cries the stall-reader, Bless us! what a word on / A title-page is this!' (Sonnet XI, lines 5–6) may be no more than a neat term for one who browses through pamphlets from the vendors' stalls, though it may carry some larger implication that the reader is too mean or too poor to buy them or to patronize properly set-up booksellers.

However, in the minor poems most words which would seem to be of Milton's coining support more comment. In 'Lycidas' 'thin-spun' neatly ties vehicle to tenor in 'Comes the blind Fury with th'abhorred shears, / And slits the thin-spun life' (lines 75–6), but it is also precisely and delicately evocative of the fragility Milton associates with human life, something so finely drawn and exiguous that it can scarcely be maintained. 'Wood-notes' in 'If . . . sweetest Shakespeare fancy's child, / Warble his native wood-notes wild' ('L'Allegro', line 132–4) is glossed by the *OED* as 'a natural untrained musical note or song like that of a wild bird in a wood': connotations cluster around it of spontaneity, of natural genius, of pastoral charm, and perhaps, too, something of the abandon of the wild wood. Woods, of course, figure as the setting for several Shakespearian comedies, so we may detect within the riot of association a literary allusion of some precision, as editors have sometimes noted.[33]

Milton's interest in psalmic settings spanned several decades of poetic creativity. His earliest extant poem, 'A Paraphrase on Psalm cxiv', on his own account written when he was fifteen and before he had learned Hebrew,[34] offers a couple of neologistic flourishes. What the Authorized Version translates as 'What ailed thee, O thou sea, that thou fleddest?' (verse 5) becomes:

> That saw the troubled sea, and shivering fled,
> And sought to hide his froth-becurled head
> Low in the earth.
>
> (lines 7–9)

Milton's coining, 'froth-becurled', amiably, if rather decoratively, extends the personification, perhaps with some precision: if the sea is a human, then perhaps froth can be conceptualized as his curly hair. However, he paraphrases markedly less felicitously the lines which the Authorized Version renders, 'Ye mountains, that ye skipped like rams; and ye little hills, like lambs' (verse 6):

> The high, huge-bellied mountains skip like rams
> Amongst their ewes, the little hills like lambs.
>
> (lines 11–12)

Here the possible neologism, 'huge-bellied', suggestive surely in seventeenth-century English of pregnancy, while it may hint at some notion of the living earth, or even of the earth as mother, rather spoils the stridently male image of the mountains as rams among ewes. Milton's much later psalmic settings, psalms lxxx to lxxxviii and i to viii, fascinating though they are prosodically and in terms of their relationship to the flourishing tradition of English psalter-writing, offer a much plainer lexis, almost unmarked by lexical interest. Perhaps one could point to what the Authorized Version renders as 'the fish of the sea, and whatsoever passeth through the paths of the sea' (Psalm 8:8): 'fish that through the wet / Sea-paths in shoals do slide' (lines 21–2), though 'Sea-paths' merely tightens up the phraseology of earlier versions.

Among the dozen or so Miltonic coinings in 'On the Death of a Fair Infant' one or two offer particular interest. For a poet of seventeen or perhaps a little older, 'long-uncoupled' is a bold innovation in his elaborate and rather mannered image of a personified and mythologized winter ravishing the lamented child to preserve the pagan gods' reputation for lasciviousness:

> [Winter] thought it touched his deity full near,
> If likewise he some fair one wedded not,
> Thereby to wipe away the infamous blot

Of long-uncoupled bed, and childless eld
Which 'mongst the wanton gods a foul reproach was held.
(lines 10–14)

The *OED* notes 'long-uncoupled' under the participial adjective 'uncoupled', where at least one of the other examples refers to marriage. Milton's usage differs rather sharply. It is not that Winter's bed has been detached or separated: rather, it has not been the scene of coupling, a distant transfer of the epithet. Again, winter slays the infant 'with his cold-kind embrace' (line 20), where the oxymoronic compound neatly points up the contradictions of the destructive appetite.

A small but eye-catching group of Miltonic coinings reflect his concern to generate, usually in a pastoral context, archaic-sounding vocabulary on the Spenserian model. Perhaps the most puzzling occurs in 'Lycidas': 'their scrannel pipes of wretched straw' (line 124). The etymology of 'scrannel', a word unrecorded before Milton and thereafter, seemingly, primarily in imitation of Miltonic usage, has puzzled commentators, though most likely it is a dialect word and as such an appropriate whiff of English provincialism and demotic usage in keeping with the decorum of pastoral. 'The pansy freaked with jet' (line 144) shows some liveliness of invention. The *OED* notes no earlier use of 'freak' as a verb. The cognate noun, about which it postulates 'possibly introduced from dialects', appears both in *The Mirror for Magistrates* and in *The Faerie Queene*, where it is used of the vagaries of fortune, a sense remote from the meaning in 'Lycidas'. Possibly Milton takes the verb from those sources; possibly he adopts it directly from unrecorded dialect usage.

A possible coining in 'L'Allegro' has associations either with folk-knowledge or else perhaps with non-standard English usage. Consider the following, which describes

> how the drudging goblin sweat,
> To earn his cream-bowl duly set,
> When in one night, ere glimpse of morn,
> His shadowy flail hath threshed the corn,
> That ten day-labourers could not end;
> Then lies him down the lubber fiend.

And stretched out all the chimney's length,
Basks at the fire his hairy strength.
(lines 105–12)

The *OED* regards 'lubber fiend' as a special combination or perhaps as discrete word, which it glosses as 'a beneficent goblin supposed to perform some of the laborious work of a household or farm during the night; a "Lob-lie-by-the fire"'. Editors sometimes relate the word to Shakespeare's epithet for Robin Goodfellow: a fairy, perhaps more spritely and ethereal than Puck himself and one who speaks banteringly to him, terms him 'thou lob of spirits' (*A Midsummer Night's Dream*, II.ii.16), where the word would seem to suggest 'bumpkin' or 'clownish fellow'. 'Lob-lie-by-the-fire' occurs in *The Knight of the Burning Pestle* in an anecdote of the Citizen's Wife, probably a fairly reliable transmitter of popular superstition: 'There's a pretty tale of a witch that had the devil's mark about her, God bless us, that had a giant for a son, that was call'd Lob-lie-by-the-fire'.[35] Unhelpfully, this is the first *OED* record of the name (under 'Lob' sb.[2], 7). Yet, just as the fairy may allude to Puck's relative clumsiness, so the Citizen's Wife may be right when she associates this name with a giant. Milton's debt to Shakespeare as a source of fairy lore and reference is clear,[36] and his 'lubber fiend' does show strength. Yet the *OED* is surely right to associate 'lubber fiend' with 'Lubber' sb., 1.c, 'An inferior servant, drudge, scullion'. The usage is a rare one – I have never encountered it – and interestingly the *OED* cites just two examples, Elyot's Latin–English dictionary of 1538, where it appears as a gloss for '*Mediastinus*', and the English dictionary of Milton's nephew, Edward Phillips, where it appears as a word to be glossed. We have some evidence that Phillips paid particular attention to some of his uncle's poetry,[37] and this may be another example. Perhaps Milton knew the usage from Elyot[38] and, prompted further by recollection of the passage from *A Midsummer Night's Dream*, was drawn to adapt it. He could not fail to have recognized that Elyot's dictionary was an old book, so the word perhaps seemed ideal for appropriation as another archaism in the Spenserian fashion.

Milton's archaizing leads him once into a familiar sort of error. In 'On Shakespeare' he asks why his bones should be hid 'Under a star-ypointing pyramid' (line 4). Strictly, the 'y-' prefix marks past participles in the Middle English period, though other archaizing poets besides Milton similarly erred in using it in the formation of other parts of verbs, including present participles.[39] Elsewhere, when he adopts the archaism, he uses it correctly ('those ychained in sleep': 'On the Morning of Christ's Nativity', line 155; 'In heaven yclept Euphrosyne': 'L'Allegro', line 12). I have further comments on Miltonic archaisms below.

The most frequent and the most characteristic kind of coining in the minor poems is the formation of compound adjectives, usually consisting of an adjective relating to colour or manner and a participial adjective, though sometimes consisting of an object or an instrument and the participial adjective relating to it. Consider, for example: 'the golden-tressed sun'; 'his thunder-clasping hand' (Psalm cxxxvi, lines 29, 38); '[Winter] mounting up in icy-pearled car'; 'that crowned matron sage white-robed Truth'; 'the golden-winged host' ('On the Death of a Fair Infant', lines 15, 54, 56); 'Sent down the meek-eyed Peace'; 'With flower-inwoven tresses torn'; 'The sable-stoled sorcerers'; 'the yellow-skirted fays'; 'their moon-loved maze'; 'Bright-harnessed angels sit in order serviceable' (On the Morning of Christ's Nativity', lines 46, 187, 220, 235, 236, 244); 'ebon shades, and low-browed rocks'; 'ivy-crowned Bacchus' ('L'Allegro', line 8,16); 'bright-haired Vesta long of yore'; 'Guiding the fiery-wheeled throne'; 'Till civil-suited Morn appear'; 'Entice the dewy-feathered Sleep'; 'To the full-voiced choir below' ('Il Penseroso', lines 23, 53, 122, 146, 162); 'Fair silver-buskined nymphs as great as good' ('Arcades', line 33); 'Sphere-borne harmonious sisters, Voice, and Verse'; ('At a Solemn Music', line 2); 'Call on the lazy leaden-stepping hours' ('On Time', line 2). I have already noted a large cluster of similarly structured epithets in *Comus*. They are not a feature of his later minor poetry. As in *Comus*, some are more complex than perhaps they seem. Thus, in the example from 'On Time', 'leaden', while a familiar epithet for clumsy or sluggish movement, links neatly with the next line, 'Whose speed is but the heavy plummet's pace' (line 3). As editors have noted, the 'plummet' or weight which controlled the operation of clocks was often made from lead and took its name from *plumbum*, the Latin for lead,[40] so the coining is particularly felicitous. 'Bright-harnessed', too, functions in a complex way. Carey argues that Milton's Nativity Ode differs from others in the genre in that it excludes the more affective trappings of the event and particularly it declines to depict the animals around the crib:

> Probably the ox and the ass are the bits of naturalness most people are sorriest to lose ... Milton leaves the animals out, and flaunts his omission. Osiris 'Trampling the unshow'r'd Grass with lowings loud' (215) can hardly help drawing attention to the gap. Nor can the 'Bright-harnessed' angels ... Of course, 'harnessed' means 'wearing armour', as it often did in the 17th century. But the word's other meaning impudently draws attention to what is not there.[41]

This is well argued, and it may be added that the association between Milton's harnessed angels and the missing beasts of the nativity is made stronger by the previous line, which discloses that they sit 'all about the courtly stable' (line 243).

Other compound neologisms are the syncopated appropriation of epithets and characteristics Milton has encountered elsewhere, the elegant absorption by the young poet of the phraseology of his masters. Editors note that the 'civil-suited Morn' of 'Il Penseroso' echoes Juliet's invocation to 'civil night, / Thou sober-suited matron, all in black' (*Romeo and Juliet*, III.ii.11–12). That dawn for the speaker of the poem should appear as soberly attired as night fits the decorum of the character, and he adds that his dawn is to be distinguished from other poetic dawns, 'Not tricked and frounced as she was wont, / With the Attic boy to hunt' (lines 123–4), an allusion to the depiction of dawn in Ovid's *Metamorphoses*.[42] Similarly, as Leishman observes, 'inweave' in the sense of 'to decorate with something inserted or entwined' has its origins in Spenser's *Muiopotmos*, in lines which seem to lie behind the 'flower-inwoven tresses' of the distraught nymphs of the Nativity Ode:

> a faire border wrought of sundrie flowres,
> Enwouen with an Yuie winding trayle.[43]

Again, Joshua Sylvester had written of 'Heav'ns Almightie' fling-
ing down 'slipperie Ice-pearls', presumably hail.[44] Milton consolidates the image in 'On the Death of a Fair Infant' into a felicitous
epithet, 'icy-pearled', for the chariot of his mythologized figure of
Winter. Such adjectival compounds disclose one aspect of the
poetic craftsmanship of the young Milton, as he absorbs, abbrevi-
ates and distils the work of his masters into his own writing.

The most remarkable aspect of these compounds, however, is
their recurrence in certain poetic environments. Persistently,
Milton uses these epithets to qualify either allegorical abstractions or mythological figures – the 'golden-tressed sun' (an incor-
poration into the psalm of a detail with a decidedly classical
quality[45]); the Christian God's 'thunder-clasping hand' and
'fiery-wheeled throne'; Winter's 'car' and Truth's robes; 'golden-
winged' and 'bright-harnessed angels'; Peace and Morn and
Voice and Verse; fays and nymphs, both flower-decked and
buskined, and the 'leaden-stepping hours'. These structures have
about them an aspect of atemporality, nor do they invite consideration of origins or purposes of the characteristics they de-
note. Who 'winged' the angels or 'suited' the Morn – and why –
are not exposed to question. Intellectually, that has a coherence.
Often Milton affixes such epithets to the entities or abstractions
which are either eternal or else abide outside the rule of time.
Truth or Peace have the transcendent immutability of Platonic
ideals. Culturally, the practice may be associated with Milton's
obvious indebtedness to the codes and conventions of renaissance
iconography. Attributes are appended to figures much as the
physical appearance and settings in renaissance figure-painting
are determined by the observation of various decorums and carry
sometimes a semantic value. In Milton's poems, God grasps his
thunder and the fays sport their yellow skirts as eternally and as
appropriately as, in renaissance art, Cupid has wings and a little
bow and the Virgin Mary wears a blue mantle.

New Senses

Sometimes words are used by Milton in what seem to be new
senses. Most are in the earlier poems, though there are a few in

his political poems of the Civil War period. Some are the attributive use of substantives. Thus 'Heaven's youngest teemed star' attends the newborn Christ 'with handmaid lamp' ('On the Morning of Christ's Nativity', lines 240, 242), an epithet which neatly suggests the sleeping child's cosmic status. Often the impulse for the semantic shift is emphatically poetic. Thus, apparently, 'fleecy' had previously meant 'covered with fleece' or 'derived from fleece' before Milton extended it in a sort of syncopated metaphor to mean 'like fleece':

> as if her head she bowed,
> Stooping through a fleecy cloud.
> ('Il Penseroso', line 71–2)

A little later 'nook' is extended to apply not to an inanimate corner or cranny or secluded region but, figuratively, to the human body conceptualized as a dwelling-place:

> The immortal mind that hath forsook
> Her mansion is this fleshly nook.
> (lines 91–2)

'Swart' was contemporaneously current as a synonym for 'black': in the phrase 'the swart star sparely looks' ('Lycidas', line 138), as editors have long noted, Milton extends its meaning to suggest not that the star (probably the dog-star) is black but that it causes other things to turn black in the singeing heat of the dog-days.[46]

Milton in *Comus*, unremarkably, extends the verb 'wreathe' from meaning 'to surround or invest with or as with something twisted or turned' (*OED* 2.a) to mean 'to encircle with a wreath or garland' (2.b): 'his clustering locks, / With ivy berries wreathed' (lines 54–5). Bolder, though, is the extension of the participial adjective in the approximately contemporary 'L'Allegro':

> Haste thee nymph, and bring with thee
> Jest and youthful Jollity,
> Quips and cranks, and wanton wiles,
> Nods, and becks, and wreathed smiles,

Such as hang on Hebe's cheek,
And love to live in dimple sleek;
Sport that wrinkled Care derides,
And laughter holding both his sides.
(lines 25–32)

The *OED* cites this as the first example of 'wreathed' meaning
'formed by wreathing the countenance' (1.c) – the word was
contemporaneously used to mean 'corrugated' or 'wrinkled'
(1.b), and applied to tree trunks and old fruit. Ingeniously,
Milton manages to have the mirthful face wrinkled by smiles but
nevertheless distinct from the wrinkled face of care, no doubt
because of the festal associations of the 'wreath' element within
it: Mirth wears its happy wrinkles like a garland. The 'dimple
sleek' momentarily puzzles: how can a dimple or dent be
'smooth'? Perhaps Milton is nudging 'sleek' in the direction of his
usage in 'on the level brine, / Sleek Panope with all her sisters
played' ('Lycidas', lines 98–9), which the *OED* cites as the first
example of signification 4, 'having a smooth skin especially as a
result of being in good condition; plump'. Certainly, Bush and
Woodhouse interpret the phrase in 'L'Allegro' thus.[47] Or perhaps
the seeming contradiction points to the nature of Mirth's dimples:
they are evanescent and resolve into smoothness as the face
relaxes.

Examples of semantic extension seem considerably rarer
among the minor poems of the 1640s and later. In 'ride us with a
classic hierarchy' ('On the New Forcers of Conscience', line 7),
Milton's 'classic' rather than the more customary 'classical' to
mean 'pertaining to a presbyterian classis' is plainly of little
significance. In Sonnet XI, his little regarded pamphlet, *Tetra-
chordon*, 'walked the town awhile, / Numbering good intellects'
(lines 3–4), which the *OED* regards as an extension of the verb
'number' to mean 'to include or comprise in a number' (7.a). The
word occurs in the Authorized Version to mean 'to collect, up to
a certain number' in the phrase 'Number thee an army' (1 Kings
20:25), so the shift is quite slight. Milton's usage suggests the
slender readership of his tract: so few read and appreciated it they
could be counted.

Unusual Collocations

As in *Comus*, Milton in his minor poetry of the early period quite frequently collocates words relating to air, the heavens and atmospheric phenomena. In the Nativity Ode Peace

>   came softly sliding
> Down through the turning sphere
> His ready harbinger,
> With turtle wing the amorous clouds dividing.
>   (lines 47–50)

'Amorous' describes usually animate creatures and their behaviour, and 'dividing', too, seems to offer a rather concrete conception of clouds' substantiality. However, the extended personification which here obtains perhaps neutralizes some of the effect. It is analogous, perhaps, to the use of 'frolic', characteristically a word used of animate subjects, in the Primavera-like description of 'L'Allegro':

> The frolic wind that breathes the spring,
> Zephyr with Aurora playing.
>   (lines 18–19)

Similarly, in a passage which animates both earth and sky, he speaks of:

> Mountains on whose barren breast
> The labouring clouds do often rest.
>   (lines 73–4)

The inanimate, let alone the ephemeral, are not customarily described as 'labouring', though of course the passage edges towards formal personification.

Carey is irked by the lines from the Nativity Ode:

> Yea truth, and Justice then
> Will down return to men,
>   Orbed in a rainbow; and like glories wearing
> Mercy will sit between,

Throned in celestial sheen,
With radiant feet the tissued clouds down steering.
(lines 141–6)

He sees a 'theatricality [which] stiffens the action, and the writing':
'we are not meant to ask how [Mercy] manages to steer clouds
with her feet. She is really sitting on clouds made of buckram, or
some such stuff ("tissued" meant "embroidered with gold or
silver thread") and would have to be lowered by stage machin-
ery.'[48] Milton, however, persistently writes of clouds and similar
intangibles in ways which attribute to them a curious materiality.
Clouds and air and light become substances to be pushed, displaced, felt and even worn. Here, Truth and Justice are 'Orbed in
a rainbow', that is encircled or enclosed by it – the 1645 version of
the poem had them wearing 'Th'enamelled arras of the rainbow',
just as in the 1673 version (Carey's copy-text) Mercy appears 'like
glories wearing', Possibly 'glories' is used here in *OED* signification 9, 'a circle of light represented as surrounding the head, or
the whole figure, of the Saviour, the Virgin, or one of the Saints',
but the usage seems not to be current for another twenty years. I
think we see, rather, the word used to mean 'resplendent beauty
or magnificence' (*OED* 6), but used within a collocation that
makes such beauty so substantial as to be worn, just as the
preposition in 'Throned *in* celestial sheen', suggests a refulgence
so bright it has dimensions of space one can inhabit. Similarly,
Milton conceives of the Marchioness of Winchester in heaven
'clad in radiant sheen, / No marchioness, but now a queen'
('Epitaph on the Marchioness of Winchester', lines 72–3).

The animation of the landscape in 'L'Allegro' finds embodi-
ment in one unusual collocation of the considerable expressive
power:

Or if the early season lead
To the tanned haycock in the mead.
(lines 89–90)

'Tanned', in the sense of browned by the sun, usually collocates
with human subjects. We might have expected it to be used of the

haymakers, but Milton transfers it to the product of their labour, which subtly suggests that the hay and workers share the same life rhythm.

Ludic Lexis

Milton's two poems on the death of Thomas Hobson, the university carrier, were printed in his own day in collections of comic verse,[49] and function through a variety of comic mechanisms, including, particularly in the second one, a number of smartly turned puns. Thus, 'Too long vacation [= idleness, university holiday] hastened on his term [= end of life, university term]' ('Another on the Same', line 14); 'his wain [= carriage; also = wane or decline] was his increase' (line 32); 'His letters are delivered all and gone, / Only remains this superscription [= address on the letter, inscription above a grave]' (lines 33–4). Other quibbles are not strictly puns, but closely adjacent to them: 'one carrier put down to make six bearers' (line 20); 'Ease was his chief disease' (line 21); 'He died for heaviness that his cart went light' (line 22), etc. Quibbles occur, too, in satirical parts of his political verse, as in:

> That so the Parliament
> May with their wholesome and preventive shears
> Clip your phylacteries, though baulk your ears,
> And succour our just fears
> When they shall read this clearly in your charge
> New *Presbyter* is but old *Priest* writ large
> ('On the New Forcers of Conscience', lines 15–20)

The metaphorical clipping of the pharisaic phylactery jumbles nicely if in grisly style with the allusion to a more literal clipping, of ears under the Laudian church-regime. The presbyter–priest quibble works on the status of 'presbyter' both as a fairly new word in English and as the word from which 'priest' is etymologically derived. Passages of sustained word-play are not elsewhere a significant element in his minor poems, though there are isolated examples. Thus, in the Nativity Ode, the 'breathed spell, /

Inspires the pale-eyed priest' (lines 179–80): the word 'inspire' is used in the sense of 'give inspiration' and simultaneously its other meaning of 'breathe into' is alluded to.

Archaisms and Related Features

Besides words he coins or borrows into literary English from possible dialect sources, early Milton in Spenserian vein adopts a number of words and usages which had seemingly dropped from currency. 'Envermeil' in 'that lovely dye / That did thy cheek envermeil' ('On the Death of a Fair Infant', lines 5–6) perhaps effects a lexical revival – the previous *OED* citation is from Lydgate. Milton's use of 'glowing' in 'The glowing violet' ('Lycidas', line 145) to mean 'brilliant, rich, and warm in colour' again probably takes an archaism from Middle English. In the same passage, 'rathe' in 'the rathe primrose that forsaken dies' (line 142) offers him a dialect word adopted by Spenserian pastoral, and 'daffadillies' (line 150) approximates to Spenser's 'daffadowndillies' at a time when the modern form, 'daffodil', was already widely current.[50] 'Unweeting' in 'with unweeting hand' ('On the Death of a Fair Infant', line 23) similarly favours a Spenserian form.[51]

Paradise Lost

Neologisms

Broadbent, who offers much good sense on the style of *Paradise Lost*, avows that 'Milton invented very few words'.[52] However, by 'invented' he seems to mean something specific if undefined, 'formed *ex nihilo*' or 'formed from non-English components', and by 'few' he seems to mean 'few in comparison with the fertility of Shakespeare's lexical inventiveness'; thus qualified, both notions are true enough, but then Shakespeare presents an unparalleled force in the history of literary English, and certainly Milton forms new words from the current English wordstock with a readiness and a felicity which seems distinctive from immediate contemporaries.

New words are, however, markedly less frequently coined in *Paradise Lost* than in *Comus*. I have noticed fewer than twice as many as in his masque, though it is ten times the length. Milton's rate of coining appears closer to that of *Samson Agonistes* or *Paradise Regained*. We may only guess, but I suspect that the reasons, in so far as they are open to surmise, lie not in an atrophy of Miltonic creativity but rather a shift both in the rate at which words were entering the language in general and a change in the prevailing poetic aesthetic away from an Elizabethan exuberance to a neoclassical austerity.

Milton seems particularly free in the formation of words through a negative prefixation. Of Belial's anxieties lest the fallen angels be condemned to a worse hell,

> There to converse with everlasting groans.
> Unrespited, unpitied, unreprieved.
>
> (II.184–5)

Fowler remarks that Milton is 'fond of this scheme, in which asyndeton (omission of grammatical connections) is combined with similarity or sameness of prefix' (*Poems*, p. 516). He cites analogues from Sophocles, Spenser and Shakespeare. For Milton, however, the collocation of terms with the same prefix – particularly 'un-' – becomes a sort of stylistic motif. Occasionally there are four elements:

> unmoved,
> Unshaken, unseduced, unterrified
> His loyalty he [Abdiel] kept;
>
> (v.898–900)

sometimes three:

> [Grace] Comes unprevented, unimplored, unsought;
>
> (III.231)

and very frequently two:

> As he [Satan] supposed, all unobserved, unseen,
> (IV.130)

> Lest . . . he [Adam] pretend
> Surprisal, unadmonished, unforewarned,
> (V.244–5)

> [Satan resolved to] leave
> Unworshipped, unobeyed the throne supreme,
> (V.669–70)

> in fight they [the good angels] stood
> Unwearied, unobnoxious to be pained.
> (VI.403–4)

Reiteration of words thus prefixed is not always asyndetic, however, though we often find something of note, an element of phonetic or syntactic patterning, as in:

> Reaping immortal fruits of joy and love,
> Uninterrupted joy, unrivalled love,
> (III.68–9)

or the beautifully constructed:

> with what pain
> Voyaged the unreal, vast, unbounded deep,
> (X.470–1)

with an alliterative pattern like a felicitous cynghanedd.

The coupling of terms, usually adjectives, beginning with 'un-' appears frequently in Milton's vernacular prose, usually with a copula, as in 'any ungenerous and unbeseeming motion' (*Reason of Church-Government*, *CPW*, I.842) or 'tyrannie unpraised or uncelebrated in a written monument' (*Readie and Easie Way*, *CPW*, VII.421). Very occasionally, the structure is asyndetic, as in 'Shrubbs, unpickt, unchosen, those are the Fathers' (*Prelatical Episcopacy*, I.626). He does not seem to combine more than two terms. So the more developed version of the scheme, offering a certain flourish or finality, perhaps functions as a marker distinguishing the language of Miltonic poetic discourse.

Milton's enthusiasm for such compounds fascinates – why

should he, more than most, define what is by what is not? – and it
produces the formation of many words previously unrecorded in
the *OED*, such as 'unreprieved' (II.185), 'unhoard' (IV.188),
'unfumed' (V.349), 'unlibidinous' (V.449), 'ungraceful' (VIII.218),
'unhide-bound' (X.601), 'unbesought' (X.1058), 'unculled' (XI.436),
words which require no great genius in the coining, for the most
part – in a sense, they existed potentially within the vocabulary of
the language, awaiting animation – but their frequency points
further to Milton's interest in these terms.

He coins several words by affixing the prefix 'self-', a feature of
Paradise Lost as of *Samson Agonistes* and an index of the poet's
further concern with individual responsibility and individual
choice and with self-regard and analysis. Hence the neologisms
'self-tempted, self-depraved' (III.130), 'self-begot' (V.860), 'self-
knowing' (VII.510) and the unrecorded 'self-left' (XI.93).

Other coinings through compounding and affixation which may
be Miltonic include such unremarkable words as 'straw-built'
(I.773), 'Hell-doomed' (II.697), 'double-formed' (II.741), 'cany'
(i.e. made of cane) (III.439), 'half-rounding' (IV.862), 'over-
woody' (V.213), 'fourfold-visaged' (VI.845), 'oary' (i.e. like oars)
(VII.440), 'auditress' (VIII.51), 'Sin-born' (X.596), 'inabstinence'
(XI.476) and 'ensanguined' (XI.654): the list is illustrative, not
exhaustive. It shows, I suppose, something of Milton's commit-
ment to brevity of expression. He seems at once precise and
somehow masterful, confidently and elegantly making from the
language what his genius requires. Some have been widely imitated. 'Embrowned', in 'where the unpierced shade / Embrowned
the noontide bowers' (IV.245–6), is used by Pope, Thomson,
Young, Dyer and Scott, and appears in at least two English
translations of Dante.[53] Some compound adjectives merit more
attention. Milton occasionally produces adjectival terms redolent
of that common feature of *Comus* and other early poetry. Indeed,
'sable-vested Night' (II.962) perhaps stirs recollection of the
'sable-stoled sorcerers' who bear Osiris's ark in the Nativity Ode
(line 220). Like many similarly structured adjectives of the early
poetry, it is used as an attributive of a personified abstraction.
The damned are 'by harpy-footed Furies haled' (II.596), an
ephitet which neatly effects the synthesis of the Furies or Eume-

nides with the claw-footed Harpies, whom Dante had included in his hell.[54] Raphael's third and lowest pair of wings

>   his feet
> Shadowed from either heel with feathered mail
> Sky-tinctured grain.
>
>   (v.283–5)

'Sky-tinctured', tinctured or dyed to the hue of the sky or perhaps even tinctured by the sky, seems a fitting attribute for the sky-dwelling seraph and ties the material description to its symbolic implications. Again, the poet asks of the vision of Death's horrors

> Sight so deform what heart of rock could long
> Dry-eyed behold?
>
>   (xi.494–5)

The previously unrecorded compound epithet seems curiously disconcerting in collocation with the metonymic 'heart': characteristically, hearts are said to feel, rather than see, nor, literally, do they have eyes.

Sometimes, the new word brilliantly syncopates an image which may be more fully rehearsed elsewhere. Satan chides Gabriel thus:

>   thou with thy compeers,
> Used to the yoke, draw'st his triumphant wheels
> In progress through the road of heaven star-paved,
>   (iv.974–6)

a concept which recurs elaborated in 'A broad and ample road, whose dust is gold / And pavement stars' (vii.577–8). Again, in *Paradise Regained*

>   a fiery globe
> Of angels on full sail of wing flew nigh,
> Who on their plumy vans [i.e. fans] received him [Christ] soft.
>   (iv.581–3)

In *Paradise Lost*, the image occurs condensed in a compound as

Satan 'At last his sail-broad vans / . . . spreads for flight' (II.927–8).

Milton's neologizing, in *Paradise Lost* as elsewhere, frequently takes the form of using words established within the vocabulary of English in new syntactic roles. Nouns become adjectives – 'torrent fire' (II.581) – or are used to form participial adjectives, as in 'squadroned angels' (XII.367). Adjectives form nouns, as in 'heavenly choirs the hymenean sung' (IV.711) or 'the length of this terrene' (VI.78). In 'through the palpable obscure find out / His uncouth way' (II.406–7), as Satan evokes for his infernal audience the prospective horror of traversing chaos, readers too are left groping for some familiar substantive to fix upon: we find instead the shaky premiss of a new noun, either the 'obscure', which is palpable, or, if the usual order is inverted, as well it may be, the 'palpable', which is obscure! Milton's most characteristic reapplication, however, is the use of participles as participial adjectives, with which *Paradise Lost* abounds, as in 'imitated state' (II.511), 'the trading flood' (II.640), 'a bannered host' (II.885) or 'tedded grass' (IX.450).

None of the neologizing practices so far considered is in any way a violation of the customary ways in which the vocabulary of English expands, nor does Milton in the process of such word-formation draw upon any words not already current in the language. Quite rarely, Milton does borrow words into English from foreign tongues, from Latin, from Greek, or perhaps from Italian.

Usually, when Milton thus adopts words into English, cognate terms are already in current use. Thus, a row of seraphim 'Stood ranked . . . / . . . to displode their second tire [i.e. volley] / Of thunder' (VI.604–6). Milton presumably borrows the form 'displode' from the Latin *displodere*, 'to burst asunder', but 'displosion' was sufficiently current for Blount to have glossed it in the first edition of his *Glossographia, or a dictionary interpreting such hard words . . . as are now used* (London, 1656), and the *OED* records its usage in technical writing of the Restoration period. Milton's coining was adopted by Swift and other writers of the eighteenth century. 'Explode', the word which subsequently has largely displaced it, was current, though only in those senses which relate to jeering from the stage. In similar fashion, he forms 'congratulant' (X.458), seemingly from *congratulantes*, the plural present participle of the Latin verb from which 'congratulate' is formed. Both the stem verb and the suffix '-ant' were thoroughly established in contemporary English. The coining forms no barrier to understanding and may perhaps have been suggested to him by the closely analogous form 'triumphant', which occurs six lines later. Milton's variant form allows him to meet the exigencies of his metre as the more obvious 'congratulating' would not. The Latinate coining in 'Silence, ye troubled waves, and thou deep, peace, / Said then the omnific Word' (VII.216–17) merely completes a set of similar divine attributes ('omniscient', 'omnipotent' and the related substantive 'omnipresence' and 'omnipotence') which occur frequently in Milton's writing and in contemporary theological English. Milton coins as an epithet for Death's mace the neologism 'petrific' (X.294), but 'petrify' and 'petrification' were well established.

Sometimes the term borrowed invokes recollection of some other cultural context. In

> him [Satan] round
> A globe of fiery seraphim enclosed
> With bright emblazonry, and horrent arms
> (II.511–13)

'horrent', 'bristling', perhaps proposes a Virgilian intertext, 'mille rapit densos acie atque horrentibus hastis' (*Aeneid*, X.178) ('he hurries on a thousand men, densely packed, in battle formation and with bristling spears'): it thus prepares us for the section very shortly afterwards in which the fallen angels play out the games of classical epic.[55] Milton's descriptions of military manoeuvres, which frequently invoke classical models, serve the decorum of neoclassical epic which in part *Paradise Lost* works to define.[56] Again, the angelic chorus hymns the Creation with the words:

> Witness this new-made world, another heaven
> From heaven gate not far, founded in view
> On the clear hyaline, the glassy sea.
> (VII.617–19)

Note the way in which Milton, as if recognizing the difficulty of the new word, glosses it immediately ('the glassy sea'); much as Shakespeare had glossed 'this hand will rather / The multitudinous seas incarnadine' with 'Making the green one red' (*Macbeth*, II.ii.60–2). For the knowing reader, however, Milton's neologism shows a singular felicity. It occurs in Revelation 4:6, 'thalassa hyaline', 'a sea of glass like unto crystal', in the Authorized Version, in a passage which describes the expanse before God's throne in a vision of heaven. The angels, who are explicitly looking towards earth from heaven and are regarding something unfamiliar to them, describe it in terms of that which is familiar to them and in vocabulary appropriate to them. Perhaps Milton is further equating the expanse on which earth and the heavenly bodies are 'founded' with the expanse described in the Book of Revelation.

The progress of 'horrent' in the language – it was sometimes imitated[57] – possibly owed something to the currency of cognate terms such as 'horrid' (which contemporaneously meant 'bristling') and 'abhorrent', and *horrere* had been borrowed into Middle English in the form 'horrend', though presumably it did not persist into the early modern period. 'Hyaline' is recorded in an example from 1661 in an adjectival usage, meaning 'resembling glass', though the word was rare, if indeed it achieved any currency.

A few of Milton's neologisms show an element of playfulness. Thus, the borrowing 'gurge', meaning 'whirlpool', which the characteristically sceptical Fowler is prepared to entertain as 'almost certainly a Latinism',[58] adapted from the Latin *gurges*, fits well into its place in the description of the siting of Babel on 'The plain, wherein a black bituminous gurge / Boils out from under ground' (XII.41–2). Its alienness felicitously anticipates the fissuring of the common language as Babel falls. Again, Milton first quibbles on the folk-etymology of the word 'pontifex' as he describes Sin and Death's construction of a bridge from earth to hell as wrought by 'wondrous art / Pontifical' (X.313–14), which suggests an equation between Satan's grim offspring and the Pope. The joke seems so good that unusually he shortly afterwards repeats it, coining on the model of 'edifice' a new word 'pontifice', 'bridge', which once more offers a quibble with the already current word 'pontifice', an epithet of the Pope: Satan meets Sin and Death 'at the brink of chaos, near the foot / Of this new wondrous pontifice' (X.347–8). The coining from Greek of 'Pandaemonium' as a place-name for 'the high capital / Of Satan and his peers' (I.756–7), while its meaning is obvious enough – both the 'pan' and the 'daemon' components had currency in other English words – makes it sound suitably grand and remote and avoids the folksiness of a coining from the native resources of English.

New Senses

Apart from Latinisms, both real and imputed, which I discuss shortly, I have noted about seventy occasions in *Paradise Lost* on which Milton extends or shifts the semantic range of words already current in English; as in *Paradise Regained*, there are decidedly fewer of these than in *Comus*. Many examples simply manifest a now familiar Miltonic energy, pushing against the syntactic or collocational restraints that contemporaneously obtained. The customary idiom was for the tongue to troll or for someone to troll *with* the tongue: Milton uses the verb transitively, apparently in such a sense for the first time, in 'To dress, and troll the tongue, and roll the eye' (XI.620). The verb occurs transitively in other senses, and Milton's phrase produces a felicitous parallel between 'troll the tongue' and 'roll the eye'. More interestingly, in

> on a sudden open fly
> With impetuous recoil and jarring sound
> The infernal doors, and on their hinges grate
> Harsh thunder
>
> (II.879–82)

Milton uses transitively 'grate', which previously, in the senses relating to the emission of sound, had been used only intransitively. Other transitive uses relate to the abrasion or excoriation of something material, and Milton's use perhaps hints at that: the thunder is materially transformed by the action of the doors of hell. The *OED* records many seventeenth-century examples of the use of 'subduct', meaning 'to take away' or 'subtract'. The example from Milton, in which Adam describes how, in the creation of Eve, nature 'from my side subducting, took perhaps / More than enough' (VIII.536–7), is the first in which the word is used intransitively. Other similar deviations show Milton using adjectives in what the *OED* terms a 'quasi-adverbial' manner. Thus, Adam and Eve appear 'erect and tall, / Godlike erect, with naked honour clad' (IV.288–9), in which the primary role of 'Godlike' seems to be to qualify 'erect'. Similarly, there is something of an adverbial force to 'pushed / Oblique the centric globe' (X.670–1).

Sometimes the semantic extension is produced through metonymy. 'Azure' had previously meant, among other things, the colour of sky: in 'not like those steps / On heaven's azure' (I.296–7), Milton extends it to mean the sky itself, foregrounding one of its most attractive qualities, poignant in the immediate context, since here he describes Satan walking the 'burning marl' of hell, and at the same time he avoids the quasi-pleonastic clumsiness of alternatives such as 'the sky of heaven' or 'heaven's sky'. Compare the metonymic extension of 'smooth' (to mean 'an expanse of smooth water') in 'on smooth the seal, / And bended dolphins play' (VII.409–10). In 'in at this gate none pass / The vigilance here placed' (IV.579–80), Milton puts the most pertinent attribute of the guard (Gabriel and Uriel are discussing whether Satan may have entered Paradise unseen) for the guard itself.[59]

As in other works, Milton sometimes extends into concrete significations words which previously had the status of abstracts. Satan, returning from Paradise, is seen 'Betwixt the Centaur and the Scorpion steering / His zenith' (X.328–9), which extends the meaning of 'zenith' from that of an astronomical abstraction, a point on his course, to mean the way or route to that point. God addresses Christ with:

> O thou in heaven and earth the only peace
> Found out for mankind under wrath, O thou
> My sole complacence!
>
> (III.274–6)

The use of 'peace' to mean 'author of peace' is Pauline: Ephesians 2:14 'For he is our peace, who hath made both one, and hath broken down the middle wall of partition between us.' On its model, Milton neatly extends the previously abstract 'complacence' to mean 'source of complacence'. Other examples, however, are doubtful and infrequent.

Milton sometimes shifts signification through a kind of metaphoric extension. Eve goes 'Not unattended, for on her as queen / A pomp of winning graces waited still' (VIII.60–1). 'Pomp' had literally denoted a train or procession. Milton, the old republican, defines the nature of true majesty, Eve's naked majesty which comes attended not by lackeys but by the native graces which she embodies. 'To mantle' had meant 'to cover or clothe in or as in a mantle'; Milton three times in *Paradise Lost* uses it or participial adjectives derived from it in a looser, more figurative way. Presumably in allusion to its habit of growth, he has 'the mantling vine' lay its grapes over 'umbrageous grots and caves' (IV.257–8).[60] In

> the swan with arched neck
> Between her white wings mantling proudly, rows
> Her state with oary feet
>
> (VII.438–40)

'mantling' seems to suggest that the swan wears its wings as an oarsman may wear a cloak over her shoulders: Milton's swan, like the citizen-rowers of classical Greek galleys, may conduct herself 'proudly', unlike the slaves of Roman or renaissance galleys, whose shoulders are naked to their masters' whips. The term further consolidates the personification implied in 'oary', 'rows' and 'state'. Democratically, though, the swan provides her own propulsion for her stately progress. Wings are again conceived as 'mantling' in Milton's description of the seraphic Raphael:

> the pair that clad
> Each shoulder broad, came mantling o'er his breast
> With regal ornament,
>
> (V.278–80)

which transforms its source in Isaiah's description, 'with twain he covered his face, and with twain he covered his feet' (Isaiah 6:2), into something appropriately decorous for his status.

Milton in 'Lycidas' had in his personification of the River Cam written of 'his mantle hairy, and his bonnet sedge' (line 104), another interesting figurative use of the word 'mantle', albeit in its substantive form. The hairiness of nature finds more striking expression in the paradisal hill:

> the champaign head
> Of a steep wilderness, whose hairy sides
> With thicket overgrown, grotesque and wild,
> Access denied.
>
> (IV.134–7)

As critics have noted, the conjunction of 'head' with 'hairy sides' effects a neat personification: as in the lines from 'L'Allegro', 'Mountains on whose barren breast / The labouring clouds do often rest' (lines 73–4), some large geomorphic formation is equated with a living creature. Despite the tonsure implied in 'champaign', 'hairy sides' hints at something inhumanly gigantic. Perhaps we recall the lubber fiend basking 'his hairy strength' ('L'Allegro', line 112).

Not all of Milton's semantic extensions work towards a more poetic expression. On a few occasions, he uses words current in English and formed from the native stock in senses which are closer to what their etymology would suggest than was contemporaneously customary. 'Palmy' had acquired the larger senses of 'triumphant' or 'flourishing': Milton uses it to mean 'covered with palms', in the phrase 'palmy hillock, or the flowery lap / Of some irriguous valley' (IV.254–5). 'Unessential' contemporaneously meant 'unimportant': Milton, with considerable precision, uses it as an epithet for eternal formlessness of night as Satan enters 'the void profound / Of unessential night' (II.438–9) – God has given no essential form to night.

The sorts of semantic extension Milton effects in *Paradise Lost* often have considerable local effect: such shifts, however, seem rather less a part of the poetic creativity than in the texturing of his early poems.

Latinisms

Eighteenth-century critics and editors left to a credulous posterity a considerable legacy of comment and annotation which attributed to Milton a penchant for using words of Latin origin in senses which are redolent of their classical signification rather than their current English meaning. Such supposed 'Latinisms' have traditionally been invoked to substantiate claims for Milton's unEnglishness and to support an adverse assessment of his achievement. Such a view cannot survive the scrutiny of a more assiduous scholarship founded on the resources of historical lexicography. Most influential, Fowler's edition of *Paradise Lost* clears out a clutter of inherited commentary, or, to adapt his own image, exorcizes 'innumerable ghost Latinisms, which were raised by early editors and superstitiously believed in by their successors'.[61] The phrase 'not a Latin sense' runs like a leitmotif through Fowler's annotation. The transformation in scholarly perception has largely been accomplished: only a score or so of 'Latinisms' or words 'used in the Latin sense' survive into the annotation of Campbell's useful edition designed primarily for an undergraduate readership.[62] What has disappeared are those cases where Milton uses words of Latin origin in senses which were contemporaneously current in English and which correspond to Latin usage but which had, by the commentators' time, passed from currency. Where the editors' knowledge of Latin surpasses their knowledge of seventeenth-century English they have simply duped themselves.

The remaining examples, while scarcely a major component of Milton's linguistic practice, often show that neatness and felicity which characterize his extensions of semantic range.

The language of English literature had been in a complex and shifting relationship with Latin and particularly with the language of the Latin literary canon at least since the fourteenth century. In Milton's age, the rising cultural ideology of neoclassicism intersected with classical cultural models with a renewed vigour. To contextualize Milton's practice properly in his most obviously neoclassical writing (and pre-eminently in *Paradise Lost*), there is a need for a study of how English neoclassical writers antecedent to Milton, particularly perhaps Jonson and Chapman, indicated their cultural affinities through formal and linguistic aspects of their poetry. Milton, in my view, operated always from a clear awareness of distinctions between English and Latin usage. In poetic discourse a certain Latinizing tendency, though of a rather particular and muted kind, is apparent in Milton as in predecessors and contemporaries. Words do find a currency in English poetry in senses they had in Latin but which they had either lost since their adoption into English or else which had not previously been associated with their English usage. But repetition of the 'Latin' sense in English poetry fixes those significations in the vernacular and eventually neutralizes their strangeness. I have considered above how Milton cleverly revitalizes 'liquid', a word which by his day had become fairly familiar in English poetry in the sense of 'clear, transparent, bright', a sense it often had in Latin poetry.[63] 'Error' had been used by Daniel and Jonson, among others, in its etymological sense of 'wandering' or 'straying about', though the *OED* suggests that it would have been felt as 'a conscious imitation of Latin usage'. Perhaps so. In Milton's description of the waters of the earth 'With serpent error wandering' (VII.302), the word functions with a singular felicity, obliquely foreshadowing, in conjunction with 'serpent' (that is, 'serpent-like') the Fall, as others have recognized. 'Clang' had meant in English 'the sound of a trumpet' (one of the significations of *clangor*. Milton used it of the sound of birds which 'With clang despised the ground' (VII.422), another signification of the Latin word. Fowler notes, as the *OED* does not, a precedent for Milton's Latinate usage in Chapman's *Iliad*, 'By her clange they knew . . . it was a hern' (X.244).[64] Interestingly, Milton goes on to mention storks, so perhaps, as perhaps in Chapman, the word may be a metaphoric extension – a bird-cry like a trumpet, such as stork or heron may be thought to emit – as well as a Latinism. 'In procint', that is, 'ready, prepared', may have been perceived as imitation of *in procinctu*: 'War he [Abdiel] perceived, war in procint' (VI.19). Once more, however, there is an analogue in Chapman's *Iliad* (XII.89), and elsewhere.

Milton then on occasions uses such terms as others had adopted from Latin as part of the vocabulary suitable to poetic discourse,

and sometimes uses them with considerable skill. His best Latinisms (and Greekisms) are those in which he seems to invoke some
more specific recollection of the classical cultural or literary
context. Thus, the 'hyacinthine locks' of Adam (IV.301) have
long been recognized as an echo of Odysseus', likened by Homer
to a hyacinth (*Odyssey*, VI.231), and a neat marker by which
Milton lightly links his epic to a classical model through a com-
munity of heroic attributes. Again, in

> yet scarce to contribute
> Each orb a glimpse of light, conveyed so far
> Down to this habitable, which returns
> Light back to them
>
> (VIII.155–8)

the absolute use of 'habitable', as editors and the *OED* have
noted, probably echoes the Greek idiom *hay oikonmena* meaning
not only 'the inhabited (world)', but by implication 'the Greek
world'. As Raphael speaks here to answer the over-curious
Adam, the word hints perhaps at the fittingness of the world as
sole appropriate resort for human civilization and the proper
bound of human speculation: 'joy thou / In what he gives to thee,
this Paradise' (VIII.170–1).

Occasionally, recognition of a Latin or Greek meaning adds a
secondary enrichment or points up a felicity of expression. When
Satan 'Springs upward like a pyramid of fire' (II.1013), readers
may catch a momentarily puzzling 'half-pun' (in Fowler's term)
on the etymology of 'pyramid', anciently derived from *pyr*, or
'fire'. In

> Light issues forth, and at the other door
> Obsequious darkness enters
>
> (VI.9–10)

'Obsequious', since it is juxtaposed with 'issues' and 'enters',
carries recollection of its ultimate origins in *sequi*, 'to follow',
though both *obsequiosus*, its immediate source, and *obsequi*
actually relate to compliance or yieldingness and are not used to
mean 'following' or 'follow'. Adam witnesses the work of Jubal,

'the father of all such as handle the harp and organ' (Genesis 4:21):

> his volant touch
> Instinct through all proportions low and high
> Fled and pursued transverse the resonant fugue.
>
> (XI.561–3)

The metaphoric force of 'fled and pursued' is enriched by recognition of etymological connections of 'fugue' with *fuga*, both Italian and Latin for 'flight'.

Such cases, though enjoyable, are rare. Even those sceptical editors, Fowler and Campbell, so obviously and admirably committed to the Englishness of Milton, overstate the incidence and significance of Latinisms. In

> last
> Rose as in dance the stately trees, and spread
> Their branches hung wih copious fruit; or gemmed
> Their blossoms
>
> (VII.323–6)

Milton uses 'gemmed' as the Romans used *gemmare*, to mean 'to bud', and the *OED* does not record its usage thus since 1150. 'Budded (a Latinism)', glosses Campbell; 'possibly rare enough to be felt as a Latinism', offers Fowler, more tentatively.[65] Perhaps so, but we should recognize that the substantive 'gem' (meaning 'bud') is recorded in numerous prose occurrences from Wycliffe onwards. Milton's verbal use could be perceived as another manifestation of his habit of using nouns as verbs. Again, the verb 'gem' was current in the sense 'to adorn with gems'. In the context of Milton's vibrant anthropomorphism, of the trees engaged in stately dance, it may function in part as a metaphoric extension: the trees are as if bejewelled with buds.

Satan 'Fluttering his pennons vain plumb down . . . drops' (II.933) and water fowl rise 'on stiff pennons' (VII.441). Both Campbell and Fowler see in the former (and perhaps implicitly in the latter, though they have no comment) a Latinism, invoking the sense of *pennae*, 'a wing'.[66] Yet the force of the Latinism must be muted by the half-pun on 'pinion', which may mean 'wing', or on 'pen', a widely current word for 'feather', and hence, in the plural, for 'wing'. The word may also function as a metaphoric extension of 'pennon', in its sense of 'streamer', especially when collocated with 'Fluttering'.

There remain in the editions of Fowler and Campbell several supposed Latinisms which seem to me merely current English usages, though the former usually qualifies his identifications with a note of caution. Why gloss 'worth ambition' in 'my choice / To reign is worth ambition though in hell' (I.261–2) as 'worth striving for (Latin *ambitio*)',[67] when it may be interpreted naturally in a current, wholly English signification? Consider

> in his [Christ's] right hand
> Grasping ten thousand thunders, which he sent
> Before him, such as in their souls infixed
> Plagues.
>
> (VI.835–8)

Why should we interpret 'Plagues' 'probably in a Latin sense' of 'blow, wound, stroke', when, as Fowler notes, it had 'the more general current meaning' of 'afflicting visitation of divine anger'?[68] It had been used thus quite specifically of manifestations of God's anger in Bible translations and other theological contexts from Wycliffe's day to Milton's own. Campbell would claim as Latinisms 'exploding' (meaning 'hissing off stage') (X.546), though both that and a vaguer sense 'of rejecting with scorn' were both current in English, and 'equal' (meaning 'fair, equitable, just') (X.748), though it frequently had had that vernacular signification since the mid-sixteenth century.[69]

Milton was an excellent Latinist with a keen appreciation of the meaning of Latin words in classical times.[70] He appreciated, too, how those usages mutated in late Latin, in Romance languages, and in vernaculars into which they had been borrowed. There is no reason to suppose that he was ignorant of the current significa-tion in English of the words he used in his vernacular writing, and he was probably acutely sensitive to semantic shifts away from classical Latin senses. We do him no service to attribute ghost Latinisms to his art. That false perception supports notions of his unEnglishness, making him appear an opaque pedant, reeking of the inkhorn, and remote from the living language. Rather, his aesthetic sought, not to simulate, but to match, to produce works that may be regarded as equalling or transcending his classical models, but in his native tongue.

Unusual Collocations

Three kinds of collocational abnormality have a particular prominence in *Paradise Lost*: cases where such insubstantial things as air and light are juxtaposed with adjectives, verbs, even prepositions which would more usually be used with objects of a greater materiality; cases where the inanimate or the abstract occurs in contexts which would predict an animate or even human category; and finally (really a subcategory of the latter), cases in which inanimate aspects of the created world are represented as sentient.

Perfumed air assumes a particular tangibility in Milton. Satan finds the naked Eve 'Veiled in a cloud of fragrance' (IX.425). Ricks, who comments sensitively on 'the unexpected substantiality' of scents, observes, 'The veil and the cloud make the roses' scent beautifully visible.'[71] Twin impulses towards both personification and the concretization of the intangible produce particularly fine effects. Adam and Eve 'in lowliest plight repentant stood / Praying' (XI.1–2):

> To heaven their prayers
> Flew up, nor missed the way, by envious winds
> Blown vagabond or frustrate: in they passed
> Dimensionless through heavenly doors; then clad
> With incense, where the altar fumed,
> By their great intercessor, came in sight
> Before the Father's throne: them the glad Son
> Presenting, thus to intercede began.
>
> (XI.14–21)

'Dimensionless', a word not previously noted by the *OED*, emphasizes with a peculiar precision the immateriality of prayer. Yet prayers may, potentially, be 'Blown vagabond' (though theirs are not); they 'passed . . . through doors'; most tellingly they may become visible – they 'came in sight' – once 'clad with incense, where the golden altar fumed'. The immaterial incense lends a mysterious substantiality to the prayers which Christ may then present to his enthroned Father as human suitors may be presented at a royal court. As editors note, the association of incense and prayer taps a rich veins of biblical imagery.[72]

Light and shade also have a fascinating materiality. The invocation to Book III, 'Hail, holy Light . . .' (III.1–55), parallels the invocations to Book I, to the heavenly muse and spirit (I.1–26), and to Book VII, to Urania (VII.1–39), and effects an equation between Light and the spirit-muses, thus confirming its personification.[73] Not only the large abstraction, 'Light', but also particular manifestations assume a materiality. Uriel comes to earth 'gliding through the even / On a sun beam' (IV.555–6). He travels 'on' the beam as if it had substance – or at least substance enough to support the ethereality of angels. I recall how in *Comus* 'some gay creatures of the element' live '*in* the colours of the rainbow' (lines 298–9).[74] Empson debates the line with Pearce and Bentley:

'I never heard but here, that the *Evening* was a Place or Space to *glide* through. *Evening* implies Time, and he might with equal propriety say: Came gliding through Six a clock. But it's the Printer's Language: the Author gave it, *gliding through the* HEAVEN' [Bentley's suggested correction]. Pearce gives precedent for coming through the evening, and points out that the part of the earth occupied by evening *is* a place, especially to so astronomical a creature. I am glad not to have to tell them what was evidently in Milton's mind; that the angel is sliding, choosing a safe gradient, down a nearly *even* sunbeam . . . But as so often when Milton is on the face of it indefensible the line seems to absorb the harshness of its absurdity; the pun gives both Uriel and the sunset a vast and impermanent equilibrium.[75]

Much of this is sensitive, especially from Pearce, but Empson discloses the fragility of his argument for a pun with the intrusive 'nearly'. Milton does not say 'nearly even', but rather an unqualified 'even'. His Uriel, moreover, is evidently subject to the laws of commonsense physics, for he leaves on the same sunbeam once its furthermost end had declined beneath his location on earth:

[Uriel] Returned on that bright beam, whose point now raised
Bore him slope downward to the sun now fallen
Beneath the Azores.

(IV.590–2)

Had the beam been 'even' in the sense of 'level', he would not
have progressed along it. Pearce's suggestion fits well with Milton's characteristic mode of representation. Evening covers a
section of the earth as a trailing edge to the day. We may compare
'The space of seven continued nights he [Satan] rode / With
darkness' (IX.63–4), which implies that darkness, too, 'rides' over
the earth.

Darkness often has a tangibility. Satan contemplates passage to
the earth:

Who shall tempt with wandering feet
The dark unbottomed infinite abyss
And through the palpable obscure find out
His uncouth way [?]

(II.404–7)

The image is of a darkness so thick it may be touched, and as
Fowler notes, develops his earlier hope that the fallen angels may
'Purge off this gloom' (II.400), which makes not only a psycho-
logical but a material point: 'the darkness is so thick that the
devils think of washing it off'.[76]

Paradise Lost presents in the depiction of Sin and Death
Milton's most elaborate and sustained foray into the allegorical
mode. Yet besides these, a multitude of abstractions, in more
intermittent fashion, appear in collocations which would usually
predict a human agent. Paradise seems a densely peopled world:

Now came still evening on, and twilight grey
Had in her sober livery all things clad;
Silence accompanied, for beast and bird,
They to their grassy couch, these to their nests
Were slunk, all but the wakeful nightingale;
She all night long her amorous descant sung;
Silence was pleased.

(IV.598–604)

Once more shade – here, 'twilight' – covers as if materially the world. More developed, silence 'accompanies' – primarily 'is associated with' – a sleepy world. Fowler suggests a secondary meaning, that silence 'accompanies musically', which offers a Keatsian paradox of 'unheard' melodies piped 'to the spirit'.[77] Silence in turn registers pleasure at the nightingale's song.

Satan anticipates 'that destruction wide may range' through Eden (IX.134). Again, as Satan assumes a bulky stature to confront Gabriel, 'on his crest / Sat horror plumed' (IV.988–9), which may be a somewhat imprecise Homeric allusion,[78] but which seems rather to suggest that Satan carries on his helmet some active and horrific creature, much as hell-hounds skirt his daughter, Sin, or snakes writhe in place of Medusa's locks. Eve feels that 'one night or two . . . derides' their horticulture with 'wanton growth' (IX. 211) – 'derides' points to a human action (though God and the angels may also laugh), just as 'wanton', though a common enough poetic term for 'luxuriant', retains in this context a hint of personification, the sportive action of deriding nights.

As Eve eats the fruit,

> Earth felt the wound, and nature from her seat
> Sighing though all her works gave signs of woe,
> That all was lost.
>
> (IX.782–4)

It is a fitting climax to a pattern of allusion which dominates Milton's way of representing the created world – and indeed the stars and planets beyond it. Adam tells Raphael that, at the consummation of his marriage:

> To the nuptial bower
> I led her blushing like the morn: all heaven,
> And happy constellations on that hour
> Shed their selectest influence; the earth
> Gave sign of gratulation, and each hill;
> Joyous the birds; fresh gales and gentle airs
> Whispered it to the woods, and from their wings
> Flung rose, flung odours from the spicy shrub,

> Disporting, till the amorous bird of night
> Sung spousal, and bid haste the evening star
> On his hill top, to light the bridal lamp.
>
> (VIII.510–20)

Despite their solitariness, a crowded wedding feast, as populous as that of Spenser's 'Epithalamion'. Note how Eve's blushes mirror the blushes of the dawn – a complex structure, in which the metaphoric blush of nature becomes the point of comparison for the woman's wholly literal blush. The constellations are 'happy' in the sense of 'propitious', but they seem, too, to show a human warmth of emotion, as do the earth and hill in their 'gratulation', an expression of joy such as humans may feel. The 'whispering' of the wind and its projection of 'rose' and (rather solid-seeming) 'odours' from its 'wings', like the lamp-lighting of the evening star, contribute to the scheme of personification, making the marriage of Adam and Eve at once magical and (rightly, as it proves) central to the destinies of much of creation. In the garden,

> On to their morning's rural work they haste
> Among sweet dews and flowers; where any row
> Of fruit-trees over-woody reached too far
> Their pampered boughs, and needed hands to check
> Fruitless embraces: or they led the vine
> To wed her elm; she spoused about him twines
> Her marriageable arms, and with her brings
> Her dower the adopted clusters, to adorn
> His barren leaves.
>
> (V.211–19)

'Pampered', a term used of human indulgence, introduces the 'Fruitless embraces', terms which may be used of vegetable growth but which in context point to connections with human generation and prepare for the more developed metaphor of the marriage of elm and vine, which in turn functions to emblematize the renewed unity of Adam and Eve after the threat posed by Eve's dream.[79]

The habit of speaking of nature as though it were sentient or even human is pervasive, present in neat, local touches. Through 'the shaggy hill' (used by others as a poetic epithet for 'over-grown') waters rise 'through veins / Of porous earth with kindly thirst up drawn' (IV.224, 227–8). Flowers 'Reared high their flourished heads between, and wrought / Mosaic' (IV.699–700). 'Flourished heads' suggests that the plants wear a floral wreath, while 'wrought' hints at the product of human endeavour.

Milton's ways of perceiving and representing the congruities between man and nature may have seemed a foolish excrescence to some intervenient generations. Yet literary taste is in a complex relation to other ideological structures. To an age like ours, distressed by recognition of the human impact on global systems, Milton's characteristic idiom speaks with a new urgency.

Wit, Puns, Complexity and Disambiguity

The witty phrase, produced by a variety of linguistic mechanisms, characterizes *Paradise Lost* even more surely than *Paradise Regained*. Some we have already noted, such as Satan's representation as a 'pyramid of fire'. Milton's term for Aries, 'the fleecy star' (III.558), as if it were to exhibit the physical properties of an actual ram, seems puzzlingly incongruous. So, too, does Satan's meditation on how he has been

> constrained
> Into a beast, and mixed with bestial slime,
> This essence to incarnate and imbrute.
> (IX.164–6)

Critics from Bentley to Empson, Ricks and Fowler have been arrested by 'incarnate', a term most frequently used of Christ: Satan's disdain, as Fowler observes, contrasts 'with Christ's willingness to undertake the permanent incarnation of his incomparably purer essence'.[80]

Terms from church government, from religious controversy, and from politics sit curiously in Milton's epic. Adam and Eve entertain Raphael, thus:

> So down they sat,
> And to their viands fell, nor seemingly

> The angel, nor in a mist, the common gloss
> Of theologians, but with keen despatch
> Of real hunger, and concoctive heat
> To transubstantiate . . .
>   Mean while at table Eve
> Ministered naked, and their flowing cups
> With pleasant liquors crowned.
>   (V.433–8, 443–45)

'Transubstantiate' reverberates with theological connotations, as does 'ministered' – 'minister', both as noun and verb, and the cognate 'ministration' recur as the usual words for the conduct of the sacraments in *The Book of Common Prayer*. Milton's choice of terms invites us to recognize here an act of communion, an Edenic love-feast of angel and people that offers a challengingly radical aspect. No priest distinguished by ecclesiastical garments borrowed 'from *Arons* old wardrope, or the *Flamins vestry*', but rather the naked Eve; in place of the altar, set 'fortifi'd with bulwark and barricado' as a 'table of separation',[81] a simple 'table'. Milton surely relished the iconoclastic frisson. Again, Abdiel, now united with the ranks of godly angels, reproaches Satan:

>   thou seest
> All are not of thy train; there be who faith
> Prefer, and piety to God, though then
> To thee not visible, when I alone
> Seemed in thy world erroneous to dissent
> From all: my sect thou seest, now learn too late
> How few sometimes may know, when thousands err.
>   (VI.142–8)

Fowler quotes with pertinence from *Eikonoklastes*: 'I never knew that time in *England*, when men of truest Religion were not counted Sectaries.'[82] Abdiel suggests that he, too, has been perceived among the Satanic legion as a deviant sectary, though when he unites with the other godly angels their strength is apparent. The connections between the prototypical encounter of good and evil and its seventeenth-century ectype are confirmed by 'dissent', which had the specific sense of 'differ in religious

opinion': in the Restoration, 'dissent' and 'dissenter' were re-
placing alternatives as the more usual terms for nonconformist
activity. 'Synod' had been used by others to mean 'an assembly,
convention, or council of any kind', but it usually referred quite
specifically to a formal assembly of the Church of England or to a
tier of church government within a presbyterian organization.
Milton uses it once of an angelic assembly – God the Father
resolves, 'let us call to synod all the blest' (XI.67). Elsewhere, in a
way the radical reader may savour, Milton uses the word of
Satanic councils (II.391; VI.156).

We have considered already a number of puns or half-puns in
Paradise Lost, witty quibbles like that on 'pyramid of fire'.
Besides such muted examples, the text is marked by several florid
puns, some of which have achieved critical notoriety. Most occur
in dialogues in which an advantage of power or knowledge is at
issue, and the jokes are sometimes grisly. As Sin and Death enter
to plunder Paradise, the former counsels:

> Thou therefore of these herbs, and fruits, and flowers
> Feed first, on each beast next, and fish, and fowl,
> No homely morsels, and whatever thing
> The scythe of time mows down, devour unspared,
> Till I in man residing through the race,
> His thoughts, his looks, words, actions all infect,
> And season him thy last and sweetest prey.
>
> (X.603–9)

'Season' is a joke they may enjoy between them, meaning both to
'prepare' man for death and, grotesquely, to 'salt' or 'garnish'
him for the palate and maw of all-consuming Death. Recollection
of the words of Ecclesiastes 3:1–2, 'To every thing there is a
season . . . A time to be born, and a time to die', renders the
phrase particularly disturbing.

The most notorious puns come during the war in heaven.
Satan, 'scoffing in ambiguous words' (VI.568), calls to his adver-
saries in terms which they may interpret as irenic, while he shares
with his colleagues, who are preparing to discharge artillery, their
secret weapon, a joke at the godly's expense:

> Vanguard, to right and left the front unfold;
> That all may see who hate us, how we seek
> Peace and composure, and with open breast
> Stand ready to receive them, if they like
> Our overture, and turn not back perverse;
> But that I doubt, however witness heaven,
> Heaven witness thou anon, while we discharge
> Freely our part; ye who appointed stand
> Do as you have in charge, and briefly touch
> What we propound, and loud that all may hear.
>
> (VI.558–67)

Satan's 'gamesome mood' (VI.620) proves infectious, as Belial after the bombardment adds:

> Leader, the terms we sent were terms of weight,
> Of hard contents, and full of force urged home,
> Such as we might perceive amused them all,
> And stumbled many, who receives them right.
>
> (VI.621–4)

In Raphael's account, the scoffing of these foes assumes equal weight with the physical consequences of the new technology:

> What should they [the good angels] do? If on they rushed, repulse
> Repeated, and indecent overthrow
> Doubled, would render them yet more despised,
> And to their foes a laughter.
>
> (VI.600–3)

Evidently, enduring a plethora of bad jokes is a price the godly must pay for their temporary eclipse, but derision is a common concomitant of defeat, a point well known to any radical who survived into the Restoration. Had not Milton himself had to endure without redress Sir Roger L'Estrange's sneering pamphlet, *No Blinde Guides* (London, 1660), the title of which fairly indicates its tone and contents? Neither Milton nor Raphael suggests that the puns have any quality. Rather, with decorum, they indicate the unpleasantness of their perpetrators who, as the angel ironically observes, 'among themselves in pleasant vein / Stood scoffing' (VI.628–9).

Yet not only the Satanic party puns. As Satan approaches his destination, God the Father jokes with Christ, 'seest thou what rage / Transports our adversary' (III.80–1), which invokes their superiority of viewpoint, knowledge and power. They both see Satan coming and see how rage has worked upon him. Coolly, the pun at once asserts the transcendence of God and Christ and, as Fowler notes, alerts us to the tone of what follows directly:

> whom no bounds
> Prescribed, no bars of hell, nor all the chains
> Heaped on him there, nor yet the main abyss
> Wide interrupt can hold.
>
> (III.81–4)

As Empson recognized, that asseveration of God's impotence is a grisly joke, but God, too, may hold his foes in derision.[83] Milton himself knew how to scoff, a point well demonstrated by the sneering jokes which pepper *Colasterion* or *Eikonoklastes* or his Latin defences.

A complexity of expression sometimes leaves readers to ponder a choice of alternative interpretations. Christ shall 'sit incarnate' on God's throne because, as God says,

> thou hast, though throned in highest bliss
> Equal to God, and equally enjoying
> Godlike fruition, quitted all to save
> A world from utter loss.
>
> (III.305–8)

The 'fruit-' of 'fruition' snags our attention, but it is not a pun. Its sole meaning here is 'the pleasure arising from possession'. Again, 'quitted' must mean 'left', not 'redeemed', since the latter reading would produce at best a tautology ('redeemed all to redeem a world', perhaps), and God is talking about Christ's relinquishing of heaven. Yet the meaning emerges – and with some precision – only after an active consideration of adjacent alternatives.

The repetition of the same or cognate words in close proximity compels a nice awareness of semantic distinction. Thus, hell saw / Heaven [that is, those who dwelt in heaven] ruining from heaven [the place]' (VI.867–8). Adam advises Eve, 'I should mind [admonish] thee oft, and mind [pay heed to] me' (IX.358).[84] Eve observes, if each alone may not stand, 'Frail is our happiness, if this be so, / And Eden [the place] were no Eden [the Edenic happiness the place embodies] thus exposed' (IX.340–1). Fowler notes that 'Eden' in Hebrew literally means 'pleasure', a point which lends a dimension both to those lines and to

> A nice and subtle happiness I see
> Thou to thy self proposest, in the choice
> Of thy associates, Adam, and wilt taste
> No pleasure, though in pleasure, solitary.
> (VIII.399–402)[85]

Note, too, 'That brought into this world a world of woe' (IX.11), and 'The world erelong a world of tears must weep' (XI.627).

This kind of insistent lexical patterning pervades the poem and gives to the texture much of its challenging wittiness. Thus, the fallen angels find

> A universe of death, which God by curse
> Created evil, for evil only good,
> Where all life dies, death lives, and nature breeds,
> Perverse, all monstrous, all prodigious things.
> (II.622–5)

'For evil only good'? 'Good for evil'? – yes; in the sense of 'good for nothing'. 'Life dies, death lives' – a paradox that works through the partial personification of 'death' or through the metaphoric extension of 'lives' (to mean 'persists' or 'abides'). Such structures have a place in defining the disturbing confusions in the darkness visible of hell. Elsewhere, Milton uses them to suggest the way in which divine attributes transcend the human frame of reference. The 'almighty Father' sits 'High throned above all highth' (III.58), higher than all that we may conceive of as high. Yet the same mechanism operates at the heart of rhetoric of the damned:

> Where there is then no good
> For which to strive, no strife can grow up,
> (II.30–1)

we now return
To claim our just inheritance of old,
Surer to prosper than prosperity
Could have assured us,

(II.37–40)

how soon
Would highth recall high [lofty, proud] thoughts.
(IV.94–5)

Even the stern resolve, 'all good to me is lost; / Evil be thou my good' (IV.109–10), operates on the seminal distinction between 'good' meaning 'righteousness' and 'good' meaning 'benefit'. Much of the pleasure of reading *Paradise Lost* comes from that active process of recognizing and resolving complexity, of distinguishing and determining between alternatives, that the lexical patterning demands of its reader.

Archaisms and Technical Terms

Paradise Lost contains very few words which can with certainty be identified as archaisms: the Spenserian impulse has evidently run its course, and another cultural imperative obtains. In hell, 'the parching air / Burns frore, and cold performs the effect of fire' (II.594–5). The *OED*'s last previous record for 'frore' in any sense is 1543, though Spenser had used 'frory' (*Faerie Queene*, III.viii.35). Milton's use was widely imitated in the eighteenth and nineteenth centuries. An *OED* record of 1880 notes the currency of 'frore' in Suffolk dialect. Possibly 'frore' rather than 'frory' was a form Milton had heard, and certainly it meets the exigencies of metre. Milton ends his protracted comparison between Satan entering Eden and a thief robbing 'some rich burgher' with:

So clomb this first grand thief into God's fold:
So since into his church lewd hirelings climb.
(IV.192–3)

'Clomb' was a form which, according to the headnote to the *OED*'s account of 'climb', Elizabethan archaists affected. It serves Milton well here. He works to effect his analogy between Satan and later Satanic hirelings through a delicate mixture of antithesis and parallelism:

So clomb [Satan] [prepositional phrase]:
So [prepositional phrase] [Satan's followers] climb.

Possibly there is closer assonance in 'clomb'/'climb' than in 'climbed'/'climb'. Certainly, the mirroring looks neater on the printed page. Moreover, the seeming rusticity of 'clomb' gives an almost proverbial finality to the equation of Satan and hirelings which Milton is suggesting.

Other archaisms are hard to find. In contrast, *Paradise Lost* contains many words used in technical senses associated with astronomy, mathematics and natural sciences, some of which seem to have had only a limited usage outside technical discourse. For example, when Milton discusses the movement of heavenly bodies – a recurrent concern of the poem – he frequently adopts the precise terminology of astronomers, as befits the precision of what he is saying, words such as 'culminate' (III.617), used of a heavenly body to mean 'to reach its greatest altitude, to be on its meridian', or 'colure' (IX.66), meaning 'each of the great circles which intersect each other at right angles at the poles'. Raphael describes the apparent dance of the planets around the earth in 'wandering courses . . . / Progressive, retrograde, or standing still' (VIII.126–7).

Sometimes, the technical terms become extended metaphorically in their semantic range. Thus, Adam, trying to reassure himself about Eve's sin, invokes the mathematical notion of proportion as a sort of metaphor for the transformation which they may expect: the serpent lives to gain the higher degree of life equivalent to people, so they are as likely 'to attain / Proportional ascent' to become 'gods, or angels demi-gods' (IX.934–7). Raphael extends his account of how angels must necessarily eat to a cosmic view of how all the created universe is animated by a process analogous to the digestive process:

The sun that light imparts to all, receives
From all his alimental recompense
In humid exhalations.

(v.423–5).

Thereafter, in the spirit of one refuting a fellow scientist, Milton adds that Raphael subsequently ate the same food as Adam and Eve with 'real hunger, and concoctive heat / To transubstantiate' the food into angelic food and to excrete, perhaps by sweating, what remained in excess: 'what redounds, transpires / Through spirits with ease' (v.437–9). The terms used seem more appropriate to a scientific treatise, but the Milton that can regard with such clarity the probabilities and concomitants of angelic digestion can do so in a vocabulary of technical precision.

4

Word Frequencies

Word frequency is an aspect of style which is immediately apparent to the reader and may often shape our perception both of the kind of discourse we are considering and of the quality of the writing. Yet it has attracted far more interest among those concerned with the statistical interpretation of language than among critics. Among the former, issues both at the level of applied linguistics and at that of statistical theory have been and remain the subject of heated controversy.[1] Few critics have examined the implications of word frequency as an aspect of style, though canonical investigation had addressed the issue as forming the basis of a possible method of 'fingerprinting' to assign authorship.

Though the statistical modelling of vocabulary growth is complex, those aspects which influence the reader's perception of style may be simply stated. As we read through a text and the number of words we consider increases, then it is our expectation that the number of different words will also increase, but at a decelerating rate. New words occur less frequently as words we have already encountered are repeated. The total number of words or 'tokens' is to be distinguished from the total number of 'types', that is, different words, or vocabulary items; the relationship between types and tokens may be expressed as a ratio, the 'type–token ratio', in which the number of types is divided by the number of tokens. If a text is so segmented that increasingly large samples are considered – the first 1,000 words, the first 2,000 words, the first 3,000 words, etc. – the expectation is that the type–token ratio falls as the sample size increases. Thus, in the first 1,000-word segment, there may be 500 different words, giving a type–token ratio of 0.5; in the first 2,000-word segment, 800 different words (ratio: 0.4); in the first 3,000-word segment,

900 different words (ratio: 0.3). Differences between texts in the rate at which the ratio falls may well constitute a stylistic dimension which shapes our response to the texture.

In my study of Milton's prose style I considered the first 3,000 words of each of his tracts, together with 3,000-word samples from a control group of texts. I found that Milton's earliest pamphlets were quite sharply differentiated from his last tracts by the larger number of types they contained. Differences could be accounted for by several hypotheses: some kinds of expository technique call for the intensive reiteration and qualification of a small number of points; differences in subject-matter may play a part; a sweeping review of a wide range of historical evidence perhaps produces a different pattern of vocabulary growth from, say, close exegesis. Yet scrutiny of lists of all the words in each of the samples suggested that, whatever else may have been at work, Milton had in his earliest writing a pronounced preference for using sets of synonyms for recurrent concepts, whereas later he favours using the same words whenever a subject reappears. For example, in the first 3,000 words of *A Treatise of Civil Power* (1659) 'scripture' and 'scriptures' occur together twenty-five times, and the only other word used for holy writ is 'gospel' (*CPW*, VII.245 (twice) and 249). In contrast, in the opening 3,000 words of *Prelatical Episcopacy* (1641) Milton uses not only the recurrent terms 'Bible', 'Gospel' and 'Scriptures', but also 'holy writ', 'that sovran book', 'the pure Evangelick Manna', 'holy text' and '*Gods* word' (*CPW*, I.627, 631, 639, 651, 652).[2]

Brian Vickers has, quite fairly, questioned the structure of that aspect of my study, suggesting that the opening sections may not represent the practice of – and the reader's experience of – the whole.[3] Three thousand words, however, constituted a very large proportion of several of the tracts. Moreover, the software then available, the COCOA suite of programs, precluded the easy analysis of more subtly constructed samples. Current software – I used OCP, the Oxford Concordance Program[4] – does allow rather more satisfactory sampling procedures.

Table 4.1 shows the ways in which the type–token ratio falls as the reader works through each text. Thus, the first 1,000 words of *Comus* contain about 560 different words (ratio: 0.56), the first

Table 4.1   Type–token ratios

Number of words	Comus	PL	PR	SA	Civil War	Lusiads	Ann. Mir.
1,000	0.56	0.55	0.50	0.50	0.49	0.51	0.52
2,000	0.50	0.44	0.41	0.44	0.41	0.43	0.44
3,000	0.44	0.41	0.36	0.40	0.37	0.40	0.38
4,000	0.41	0.39	0.34	0.37	0.34	0.36	0.35
5,000	0.38	0.37	0.31	0.35	0.31	0.33	0.34
6,000	0.38	0.36	0.30	0.33	0.29	0.32	0.32
7,000	0.35	0.34	0.30	0.31	0.28		0.30
8,000		0.32	0.29	0.30	0.26		0.29
9,000		0.31	0.27	0.29	0.25		0.28
10,000		0.29	0.27	0.28			
11,000		0.29	0.26	0.27			
12,000		0.28	0.26	0.27			
13,000		0.27	0.25				
14,000		0.26	0.25				
15,000		0.26	0.24				
16,000		0.25					

2,000, about 1,000 different words (ratio: 0.5), the first 3,000, approximately 1,320 different words (ratio: 0.44). Except for *Paradise Lost*, I have analysed almost the whole of each of Milton's longer poems, and I have also considered the whole of Dryden's *Annus Mirabilis*, the first two books of Cowley's *The Civil War*, and the first canto of Fanshawe's translation of *The Lusiads*, the same texts used as controls in chapter 2. The sort of confluence in ratios which occurs over the higher values makes for distinct difficulties in the interpretation of that part of the table. Over the first 6,000–7,000 words, however, the figures disclose a distinction which probably indicates well the differences in texture which a reader may discern. *Comus* shows the largest number of vocabulary items; *Paradise Lost* closely approaches it; both are distinct from *Samson Agonistes* and *Paradise Regained*, which in this respect more nearly resemble the non-Miltonic texts. Differences between Milton's poetry and his prose are quite pronounced, as a comparison of the first

3,000-word segments of poems and tracts discloses. The lowest type–token ratio for a prose work, *Civil Power*, is 0.28, the highest, *Animadversions*, is 0.38, which is higher than *Paradise Regained* but lower than the other poems. Type–token ratio probably constitutes a genre characteristic, or, rather, a characteristic which distinguishes poetic discourse from prose.

Yet as in the case of Milton's prose, distinctions between his poems in terms of type–token ratio can at least in part be accounted for by shifting preferences in the use of synonyms and in the repetition of the same words for recurrent concepts. For example, in *Comus* there are numerous references to the sylvan setting. Milton uses the words 'wood' and 'woods' together thirteen times, but he seems at pains to produce alternative phrases from the same semantic field, such as 'these brakes and trees' (line 147), 'the blind mazes of this tangled wood' (line 180), 'this leafy labyrinth' (line 277), 'this tufted grove' (line 224), 'this gloomy covert wide' (line 944), etc. Thus, in

> I know each lane, and every alley green
> Dingle, or bushy dell of this wild wood,
> And every bosky bourn from side to side
> (lines 310–13)

Milton rings changes on several semantically cognate terms, 'dell' and 'dingle', 'bushy' and 'bosky', 'lane' and 'alley'. Such texturing is untypical of *Paradise Regained* and *Samson Agonistes*, both of which are characterized by the reiteration of several thematically or narratively central terms. In the latter, for example, several nouns recur frequently – 'death' (eighteen times), 'life' (twenty-three times), 'strength' (thirty-nine times), 'man' and 'men' (forty-seven times), 'God' (fifty-four times). The dating of the play has been a heated area of debate.[5] Of course, a consummate artist in control of his style can change aspects only to change them back again. Nevertheless, the affinities here between *Samson Agonistes* and *Paradise Regained* are very close, and perhaps to some may suggest a proximity in their date of composition.

Conclusions

The language of Milton's political prose mutated in straightforward ways over the thirty-two-year period of his writing. Syntactical structures remained largely unchanged, except for those in *Of True Religion, Heresy, Schism, and Toleration* (London, 1673), written thirteen years after his penultimate pamphlet. But from 1641 to 1660 his lexical practices simplified markedly. The playfulness, the exuberant creativity of his earliest writing gave way to what I have termed 'a spare functionalism'.[1] The style of his poetry discloses differences of a subtler kind, which cannot so readily be schematized. Syntactically, *Comus* in most respects shows more affinities with the epics and with *Samson Agonistes* than with his other early poetry. All the minor verse exhibits a syntactical simplicity which is closer to the norms of seventeenth-century poetic practice than to the characteristic complexity of Milton's longer poems, which have pronounced similarities in their sentence structure with the habits of his prose. Like his pamphlets, his longer poems have many long sentences produced by the multiplication of subordinate clauses. Such sentences are in no way alien or unEnglish. The result is both precision of qualification and an argumentative and cohesive power which are probably unique within the English poetic tradition. Yet Milton is a master at varying his texture. In *Paradise Lost*, at least, narrative modes are syntactically differentiated from dialogue, and throughout the oeuvre he produces short sentences of a telling simplicity.

All the early poetry owes much to the influence of certain Elizabethan models, and it is marked, too, by a strong propensity for neologizing and for semantic extension. Those influences and that propensity later fade. Yet other riches remain common

throughout, in a lexis characterized by innovation, wit and precision. Changes in texture over his career may relate, I feel, to his
cardinal status in the history of English cultural ideology, as
perhaps the last major poet of its literary renaissance, heir to
Spenser and Shakespeare, and, in his later work, the most influential of neoclassicists and the recurrent model for the poets of
the eighteenth century. Yet, throughout, Milton's vernacular
poetry is rooted profoundly in the resources of English, however
later critics may have misperceived it.

I have not sought to disguise my partisanship for Milton's
poetry. My work originates in my belief in its astonishing quality,
surpassed in English only by Shakespeare. I am aware, too, of my
partisanship for a way of reading and a mode of critical response
out of step with new orthodoxies. That tag of Valéry, 'Every
work is the work of many things besides an author', elevated by
Eagleton to the status of an epigraph,[2] offers a seminal insight,
and I have laboured to situate Milton's text in relationship both to
the literary and cultural intertext and to the English language in
the mid-seventeenth century. But 'besides an author' does not
mean 'instead of an author'. I have persistently felt the intelli-
gence, precision and control of Milton's creative genius. If this
work has a larger purpose, it is the celebration of Milton as
maker.

Yet numerous questions remain, some awaiting resolution
within a different investigative framework, others depending on
technological innovations of an imminent or remote kind. For
example, I have differentiated the relationship of syntax to lineation both between different parts of the Milton canon and between Milton and an appropriate sample of contemporary poets.
An analysis focused on this aspect of style but covering a wider
range of periods and genres (including, say, dramatic poetry)
could well contextualize Milton's practice rather differently and
disclose both antecedents, parallels and his possible influence.
The notion of Milton's use of Latinisms raises large and interesting questions about the cultural ideology, neoclassicism, and the
ways in which it is inscribed in literary texts of the seventeenth
century. Again, only eclectically and with difficulty could a
computer-readable version of Milton's poetry be assembled for

this study, and the costs and problems of data-preparation restricted me to the construction of only a rudimentary control corpus of contemporary writing. Milton is served no worse than all but a handful of English writers, and rather better than most, and archives, pre-eminently the Oxford Text Archive, have laboured to preserve and make accessible what has been transcribed into an electronic medium. Clearly, the preparation of editorially sound versions of canonical English writers is an urgent and realizable objective for academic collaboration, and the large corpora which would be produced would permit surer identification in specific texts of areas of collocational and registral abnormality, neologizing and archaism, and would facilitate the recognition and interpretation of allusion and influence. The online version of the *OED* permits a readier and more exhaustive access to the information it contains, though one must operate largely within horizons set by nineteenth-century lexicography, a problematic which excludes a proper consideration of many issues of importance. Systems which will permit the rapid interrogation and analysis of very large databases of appropriate texts would make possible a precise approach to questions which relate to frequency and probability and to more recently developed categories of linguistic analysis. The provisionality, then, of this study – and perhaps all such studies – is inescapable while our knowledge both of the norms of seventeenth-century poetic practice and of the achievements of its towering figures remains uncertain and incomplete.

Notes

Chapter 1 Milton Studies: Past, Present and in Prospect

1 William Empson, *Milton's God*, 1st edn (London, 1961; 2nd edn, London, 1965); *The Poems of John Milton*, ed. John Carey and Alastair Fowler (London, 1968; second impression with corrections, London, 1980).
2 Christopher Ricks, *Milton's Grand Style* (Oxford, 1963); Ronald David Emma, *Milton's Grammar* (The Hague, 1964); Stanley Eugene Fish, *Surprised by Sin: The Reader in Paradise Lost* (London and New York, 1967).
3 Samuel Johnson, 'Life of Milton', in *Samuel Johnson*, ed. Donald Greene (Oxford, 1984), pp. 714–15.
4 For a reading of the politics of their criticism, see Chris Baldick, *The Social Mission of English Criticism 1848–1932* (Oxford, 1987; first published 1983), and on the infuence of and opposition to Eliot's views, see Robert Martin Adams, *Ikon: John Milton and the Modern Critics* (Ithaca, NY, 1955), esp. ch. 6.
5 F. R. Leavis, *Revaluation* (Harmondsworth, 1967; first published 1936), pp. 50, 49, 56.
6 T. S. Eliot, 'Milton', *Proceedings of this British Academy*, 33 (1947), p. 69.
7 T. S. Eliot, 'A note on the verse of John Milton', *Essays and Studies*, 21 (1936), p. 40.
8 William Empson, *Some Versions of Pastoral* (Harmondsworth, 1966; first published 1935), pp. 121–55.
9 A. J. A. Waldock, *Paradise Lost and its Critics* (Cambridge, 1947).
10 Lalia Phipps Boone, 'The language of Book VI, *Paradise Lost*', in *SAMLA Studies in Milton: Essays on John Milton and His Works* (Gainsville, Fla, 1953).
11 Richard Ohmann, 'Generative grammar and the concept of literary style', *Word*, 20 (1964), pp. 423–39; Richard Ohmann, 'Literature as sentences', *College English*, 27 (1966), pp. 261–7; J. P. Thorne, 'Generative grammar and stylistic analysis', in *New Horizons in Linguistics*, ed. John Lyons (Harmondsworth, 1970), pp. 185–97;

Roger Fowler, ed., *Essays on Style and Language* (London, 1966); Roger Fowler, *The Languages of Literature* (London, 1971).

12 T. A. Sebeok, ed., *Style in Language* (Cambridge, Mass., 1960) contains the proceedings of the 1958 Indiana conference, which is often perceived as the inception of linguistic stylistics in English; see, for example, Nigel Fabb, Derek Attridge, Alan Durant and Colin MacCabe, eds, *The Linguistics of Writing: Arguments Between Language and Literature* (London, 1987), *passim*.

13 Louis Tonko Milic, *A Quantitative Approach to the Style of Jonathan Swift* (The Hague, 1967).

14 A. C. Partridge, *The Language of Renaissance Poetry: Spenser, Shakespeare, Donne, Milton* (London, 1971).

15 J. B. Broadbent, *Paradise Lost: Introduction* (Cambridge, 1972)

16 Archie Burnett, *Milton's Style: The Shorter Poems, Paradise Regained, and 'Samson Agonistes'* (London, 1981).

17 Thomas N. Corns, *The Development of Milton's Prose Style* (Oxford, 1982).

18 Christopher Hill, *Milton and the English Revolution* (London and Boston, 1977); Andrew Milner, *John Milton and the English Revolution* (London, 1981); Michael Wilding, *Dragons Teeth: Literature in the English Revolution* (Oxford, 1987); Thomas N. Corns, '"Some rousing motions": the plurality of Miltonic ideology', in *Literature and the English Civil War*, ed. Thomas Healy and Jonathan Sawday (Cambridge, forthcoming).

19 The emergence of a predominantly Saussurian model for literary linguistics has been traced with some cogency to Roman Jakobson's contribution to the Indiana conference, 'Concluding statement: linguistics and poetics', in Sebeok, *Style*, pp. 350–77; see David Lodge, 'After Bakhtin', in Fabb et al., *Linguistics of Writing*, p. 89.

20 Margarita Stocker, *Paradise Lost: An Introduction to the Variety of Criticism* (Basingstoke, 1988).

21 The Third International Milton Symposium. Florence and Vallombrosa, 1988, selected papers from which will be published by the Medieval and Renaissance Text Society in 1989.

22 Stanley Eugene Fish, 'What is stylistics and why are they saying such terrible things about it?', reprinted in his *Is There a Text in This Class?* (Cambridge, Mass. and London, 1980), pp. 68–96; for evidence of this essay's persisting influence, consider its centrality to the stylistics debate on the HUMANIST electronic bulletin board, summer 1988.

23 Ibid., p. 72.

24 Ibid., p. 77.

25 *Poems*, p. 437.

26 Fish, 'What is stylistics . . .?', p. 17.

27 Thomas Sprat, *History of the Royal Society*, ed. Jackson I. Cope and Harold Whitmore Jones (St Louis, Miss. and London, 1966; first published 1959), p. 44.

Chapter 2 Sentence Structure

1 The sample is drawn from *Jacobean and Caroline Poetry: An Anthology* (herafter cited as *JACP*), ed. T. G. S. Cain (London and New York, 1981), pp. 78–136, 155–202, 238–99, exclusive of editorial material. I did not analyse Cain's selections from Cowley in the sample from *JACP* on the grounds that he would be well represented from elsewhere.
2 Abraham Cowley, *The Civil War*, ed. Allan Pritchard (Toronto and Buffalo, 1973), Books I and II, pp. 73–106; *The Lusiads of Luis de Camões*, tr. Sir Richard Fanshawe, ed. Geoffrey Bullough (London and Fontwell, 1963), Canto I, pp. 59–85; John Dryden, *Annus Mirabilis*, in *The Works of John Dryden*, vol. I, ed. Edward Niles Hooker et al. (Berkeley and Los Angeles, 1956), pp. 59–105.
3 The random sample was arrived at using a FORTRAN program kindly written for me by S. A. Jones, of the Computing Laboratory, University College of North Wales.
4 For an account of the suite of programs and its application, see *SPSS^x User's Guide* (New York, 1983). SPSS^x is the trademark of SPSS Inc.
5 Mindele Treip, *Milton's Punctuation and Changing English Usage 1582–1678* (London, 1970), *passim*. See also Thomas N. Corns, 'Punctuation in Milton's vernacular prose', *Notes and Queries*, n.s., 25 (1978), pp. 18–19.
6 For his prose practice, see Thomas N. Corns, *The Development of Milton's Prose Style* (Oxford, 1982), pp. 31–42.
7 A. J. A. Waldock, *Paradise Lost and its Critics* (Cambridge, 1947).
8 *PL*, IV.192–3, n.; on the change in diet of present-day predators, see *PL*, X.710–12.
9 Brian Vickers, *Francis Bacon and Renaissance Prose* (Cambridge, 1968), *passim*.
10 *PL*, I.1. n.
11 Christopher Ricks, *Milton's Grand Style* (London, Oxford and New York, 1967; first published 1963), p. 73.
12 See pp. 1–2.
13 For example, Edward S. Le Comte, '*Areopagitica* as a scenario for *Paradise Lost*', in *Achievements of the Left Hand: Essays on the Prose of John Milton*, ed. Michael Lieb and John T. Shawcross (Amherst, 1974), pp. 121–41.

14 See *Poems*, pp. 439–40, for a review of some of the issues.
15 Archie Burnett reviews some interpretations in '"Sense variously drawn out": the line in *Paradise Lost*', forthcoming.
16 John Donne, *Poetical Works*, ed. Sir Herbert Grierson (London, 1968; first published 1933), p. 7.
17 Burnett, 'Sense'.
18 *Poems*, pp. 456–7.
19 Ants Oras, 'Milton's early rhyme schemes and the structure of *Lycidas*', *Modern Philology*, 52 (1954), pp. 12–22.
20 Alastair Fowler, *Kinds of Literature: An Introduction to the Theory of Genres and Modes* (Oxford, 1982), *passim*.
21 Archie Burnett, *Milton's Style: The Shorter Poems, Paradise Regained, and 'Samson Agonistes'* (London and New York, 1981), p. 99.

Chapter 3 Lexis

1 F. R. Leavis, *Revaluation* (Harmondsworth, 1967; first published 1936), pp. 42–8. On the copious studies of the Shakespearian and Spenserian elements in *Comus* see *Var. Comm.*, pp. 762–6. Carey's headnote is particularly useful (*Poems*, p. 171).
2 Generally the best guide to whether a word is new to the language is the evidence of the *OED*. Comments on the currency and status of words which are not substantiated from other evidence are tacitly based on the *OED*.
3 *Animadversions*, CPW, I.666–7.
4 I owe this list of alternatives to Edward Le Comte, *A Dictionary of Puns in Milton's English Poetry* (London and Basingstoke, 1981), pp. 81–2. For an account of the controversy see *Var. Comm.*, II.932–8.
5 *Var. Comm.*, II.927.
6 *The Shepheardes Calendar*, 'November', line 111. See also Michael Wilding, *Dragons Teeth: Literature in the English Revolution* (Oxford, 1987), p. 64.
7 *Shepheardes Calendar*, 'May', line 36, for example.
8 Leavis, *Revaluation*, p. 48.
9 John Carey, *Milton* (London, 1976; first published 1969), p. 54.
10 Archie Burnett, *Milton's Style: The Shorter Poems, Paradise Regained, and 'Samson Agonistes'* (London and New York, 1981), p. 64.
11 *Poems*, p. 226; *Var. Comm.*, II.980.
12 For a similar point, see *Var. Comm.*, II.980.
13 Some editors have recognized an allusion to Petrarch's description of the Virgin Mary (*Poems*, p. 215; *Var. Comm.*, II.952).

14 Le Comte sees a pun on hedgehog and elf: *Dictionary of Puns*, p. 199.

15 *Poems*, p. 191.

16 For analogues from classical and renaissance poetry, see *Var. Comm.*, II.978.

17 William Shakespeare, *The Tempest*, ed. Frank Kermode (London, 1975; first published 1954), IV.i.148–56.

18 See p. 86 for other 'self-' compounds.

19 See the Choric reference to 'foreskins' (line 144), discussed on p. 60.

20 *Glossarium Mediae et Infimae Latinitatis* (Paris, 1937–8), s.v. 'obstrictio'.

21 On Milton's tribulations as a diplomatic Latinist and his attempts to reform diplomatic Latin on classical lines, see Leo Miller, *John Milton and the Oldenburg Safeguard* (New York, 1985) p. 286.

22 *Poems*, p. 347.

23 See p. 59.

24 *Var. Comm.*, IV.69–70.

25 *Poems*, p. 1156.

26 Le Comte, *Dictionary of Puns*, pp. vii, xv–xvi. He redefines the term 'pun' to include many sportive features I consider here.

27 Burnett amusingly reviews the assumptions underlying those critical accounts which regard *Paradise Regained* as plain, flat, dry, etc. (*Milton's Style*, pp. 112–31).

28 Sir Walter Raleigh, *Milton* (London, 1900), p. 211; quoted by Le Comte, *Dictionary of Puns*, p. 146.

29 *Var. Comm.*, IV.123.

30 Z. S. Fink, *The Classical Republicans* (Evanston, 1945), *passim*; *Var. Comm.*, IV.65–6.

31 *Poems*, 1079.

32 Thomas N. Corns, '"Some rousing motions": the plurality of Miltonic ideology', in *Literature and the English Civil War*, ed. Thomas Healy and Jonathan Sawday (Cambridge, forthcoming).

33 *Var. Comm.*, II.i.303.

34 According to a headnote in the 1645 edition of his collected poems (*Poems*, p. 6).

35 Francis Beaumont, *The Knight of the Burning Pestle*, ed. John Doebler (London, 1975; first published 1964), III.425–8.

36 The rest of the passage owes much to *A Midsummer Night's Dream*, II.i.32–57, as editors note.

37 W. R. Parker, letter to *The Times Literary Supplement*, 2 January 1937, p. 12.

38 Milton seems not to refer elsewhere to Elyot's dictionary.

39 *OED*, s.v. 'Y–', 3.

40 *Var. Comm.*, II.i.167–8.

41 Carey, *Milton*, p. 32.

42 *Poems*, pp. 144, 82; *Var. Comm.*, II.i.330.

43 *Muiopotmos*, lines 298–9; quoted by J. B. Leishman, *Milton's Minor Poetry* (London, 1969), p. 62.

44 *Divine Weeks and Works of Du Bartas* tr. Joshua Sylvester, ed. Susan Snyder (Oxford, 1972), 2.3.1., line 282, p. 497.

45 A mythologized sun appears, 'hastened by the golden-haired Hours' ('auricomis urgentibus Horis'), in Valerius Flaccus, *Argonautica*, Loeb edition (London, 1934), IV.92. However, editors have noted the phrase 'solem auricomum' in Buchanan's translation of the psalms (*Var. Comm.*, II.i.116–17).

46 *Var. Comm.*, II.ii.709.

47 *Var. Comm.*, II.i.30.

48 Carey, *Milton*, p. 35.

49 In *A Banquet of Jests* (London, 1640; 2nd edn, London, 1657) and in *Wit Restor'd* (London, 1658); see *Poems*, p. 125.

50 *Shepheardes Calendar*, 'July', line 78, and 'December', line 98; *Poems*, pp. 250–1.

51 *Var. Comm.*, II.i.130.

52 J. B. Broadbent, *Paradise Lost: Introduction* (Cambridge, 1972), p. 112.

53 *OED*, s.v. 'Embrown' and 'Embrowned'.

54 *Inferno*, XIII.10; *Poems*, p. 535.

55 II.528ff.: compare *Aeneid*, VI.642–59; *Poems*, p. 532.

56 See, for example, IV.785, VI.114–26, 539, 635.

57 *OED* cites, among others, Akenside and Southey.

58 *Poems*, p. 1030; *OED* cites two examples of its use as a verb in the sixteenth century.

59 *Poems*, p. 647.

60 Compare the 'green mantling vine' of *Comus*, line 294.

61 *Poems*, p. 432.

62 Campbell's edition retains the text of B. A. Wright from its predecessor in the Everyman Library, but the notes, introduction and translations are new.

63 See, pp. 57, 66.

64 *Poems*, p. 800.

65 Campbell, p. 570; *Poems*, p. 794.

66 Campbell, p. 555; *Poems*, p. 551.

67 *Poems*, p. 477.

68 *Poems*, p. 769.

69 Campbell, pp. 580–1.

70 On his classical Latinity, see Miller, *John Milton*, esp. ch. 30, though there is still work to be done.

71 Christopher Ricks, *Milton's Grand Style* (London, Oxford and New York, 1967; first published 1963), p. 95; see pp. 93–6 for other examples.

72 Ps. 141:2; Rev. 8:3, 5:8; *Poems*, pp. 982–3.

73 Whether light may be interpreted as a symbol for Christ has been and remains a focus for debate; see *Poems*, p. 559, for a summary; Walter Schindler, *Voice and Crisis: Invocation in Milton's Poetry* (Hamden, Conn., 1984), *passim*; and Michael Bauman, *Milton's Arianism* (Frankfurt am Main, Berne and New York, 1987), pp. 214–32.

74 Discussed on p. 57.

75 William Empson, *Some Versions of Pastoral* (Harmondsworth, 1966; first published 1935), pp. 129–30.

76 *Poems*, p. 526.

77 *Poems*, p. 648; John Keats, 'Ode on a Grecian Urn', in *The Poems of John Keats*, Annotated English Poets, ed. Miriam Allott (London and New York, 1970 and 1972), lines 11, 14.

78 *Iliad*, IV.441–3; *Poems*, p. 670.

79 *Poems*, p. 687.

80 Ricks, *Milton's Grand Style*, p. 73; *Poems*, p. 865; compare *Paradise Lost*, III.227ff.

81 *Of Reformation*, *CPW*, I.521, 547.

82 *Eikonoklastes*, *CPW*, III.348; *Poems*, p. 736.

83 *Poems*, p. 565; William Empson, *Milton's God*, 2nd edn (London, 1965; first published 1961), p. 119.

84 *Poems*, p. 875.

85 *Poems*, pp. 835, 874.

Chapter 4 Word Frequencies

1 See, for example, Gustav Herdan, *Quantitative Linguistics* (London, 1964), esp. ch. 10, and Charles Muller, 'Lexical distribution reconsidered: the Waring–Herdan formula', in *Statistics and Style*, ed. Lubomír Doležel and Richard W. Bailey (New York, 1969), pp. 42–56.

2 Thomas N. Corns, *The Development of Milton's Prose Style*, (Oxford, 1982), pp. 1–5, 66–8.

3 Brian Vickers, review of Corns, *Development*, *Modern Language Review*, 83 (1988), pp. 673–4.

4 For an account of the program and its operation, see Susan Hockey and Jeremy Martin, *Oxford Concordance Program Users' Manual Version 2.0* (Oxford, 1988).

5 Some of the issues are reviewed by Carey in *Poems*, pp. 330–2.

Conclusions

1 Thomas N. Corns, *The Development of Milton's Prose Style* (Oxford, 1982), p. 161; Thomas N. Corns, 'Prose', in *The Cambridge Companion to Milton*, ed. Dennis Danielson (Cambridge, 1989), pp. 183–96.
2 Terry Eagleton, *Criticism and Ideology* (London, 1976), p. 44.

Bibliography

Adams, Robert Martin, *Ikon: John Milton and the Modern Critics.* Ithaca, NY: Cornell University Press, 1955.

Baldick, Chris, *The Social Mission of English Criticism 1848–1932.* Oxford: Clarendon, 1987; first published 1983.

Banquet of Jests, A, London: 1640; 2nd edn, London: 1657.

Bauman, Michael, *Milton's Arianism.* Frankfurt am Main, Berne and New York: Peter Lang, 1987.

Beaumont, Francis, *The Knight of the Burning Pestle*, ed. John Doebler. London: Edward Arnold, 1975; first published 1964.

Boone, Lalia Phipps, 'The language of Book VI, *Paradise Lost*', *SAMLA Studies in Milton: Essays on John Milton and His Works*, ed. J. Max Patrick. Gainesville, Fla: Florida University Press, 1953.

Broadbent, J. B., *Paradise Lost: Introduction.* Cambridge: Cambridge University Press, 1972.

Burnett, Archie, *Milton's Style: The Shorter Poems, Paradise Regained, and 'Samson Agonistes'.* London and New York: Longman, 1981.

Cain, T. G. S., *Jacobean and Caroline Poetry: An Anthology* London and New York: Methuen, 1981.

Camões, Luis de, see Fanshawe, Sir Richard.

Campbell, Gordon, ed. *John Milton: The Complete Poems*, text ed. B. A. Wright. London and New York: Dent and Dutton, 1980.

Carey, John, *Milton.* London: Evans, 1976; first published 1969.

Carey, John and Fowler, Alastair, eds, *The Poems of John Milton*, Annotated English Poets. 2nd impression with corrections. London: Longman, 1980; first published 1968.

Corns, Thomas N., 'Punctuation in Milton's vernacular prose', *Notes and Queries*, n.s., 25 (1978), pp. 18–19.

Corns, Thomas N., *The Development of Milton's Prose Style.* Oxford: Clarendon Press, 1982.

Corns, Thomas N., '"Some rousing motions": the plurality of Miltonic ideology', *Literature and the English Civil War*, ed. Thomas Healy and Jonathan Sawday. Cambridge: Cambridge University Press, forthcoming.

Corns, Thomas N., 'Prose', *The Cambridge Companion to Milton*, ed.

Dennis Danielson. Cambridge: Cambridge University Press, 1989, pp. 183–96.

Cowley, Abraham, *The Civil War*, ed. Allan Pritchard. Toronto and Buffalo: University of Toronto Press, 1973.

Donne, John, *Poetical Works*, ed. Sir Herbert Grierson. London: Oxford University Press, 1968; first published 1933.

Dryden, John, *Annus Mirabilis, The Works of John Dryden*, vol. I, ed. Edward Niles Hooker et al. Berkeley and Los Angeles: University of California Press, 1956.

Du Bartas, G. de S., see Sylvester, Joshua.

Eagleton, Terry, *Criticism and Ideology*. London: New Left Books, 1976.

Eliot, T. S., 'A note on the verse of John Milton', *Essays and Studies*, 21 (1936), pp. 32–40.

Eliot, T. S., 'Milton', *Proceedings of the British Academy*, 33 (1947), pp. 61–79.

Emma, Ronald David, *Milton's Grammar*. The Hague, 1964.

Empson, William, *Some Versions of Pastoral*. Harmondsworth: Penguin, 1966; first published 1935.

Empson, William, *Milton's God*. 2nd edn, London: Chatto and Windus, 1965; first published 1961.

Fabb, Nigel, Derek Attridge, Alan Durant and Colin MacCabe, eds, *The Linguistics of Writing: Arguments Between Language and Literature*. London: Macmillan, 1987.

Fanshawe, Sir Richard, tr., *The Lusiads of Luis de Camões*, ed. Geoffrey Bullough. London and Fontwell: Centaur, 1963.

Fink, Zera S., *The Classical Republicans: An Essay in the Recovery of a Pattern of Thought in Seventeenth Century England*. Evanston: Northwestern University Press, 1945.

Fish, Stanley Eugene, *Surprised by Sin: The Reader in Paradise Lost*. London and New York: Macmillan and St Martin's, 1967.

Fish, Stanley Eugene, 'What is stylistics and why are they saying such terrible things about it?', *Is There a Text in This Class?* Cambridge, Mass. and London: Harvard University Press, 1980.

Flaccus, Valerius, *Argonautica*, Loeb edn. London: Heinemann, 1934.

Fowler, Alastair, *Kinds of Literature: An Introduction to the Theory of Genres and Modes*. Oxford: Clarendon Press, 1982.

Fowler, Roger, ed., *Essays on Style and Language*. London: Routledge and Kegan Paul, 1966.

Fowler, Roger, *The Languages of Literature*. London: Routledge and Kegan Paul, 1971.

Glossarium Mediae et Infimae Latinitatis. Paris: Librarie des Sciences et des Artes, 1937–8.

Herdan, Gustav, *Quantitative Linguistics*. London: Butterworth, 1964.

Hill, Christopher, *Milton and the English Revolution*. London and Boston: Faber, 1977.

Hockey, Susan and Martin, Jeremy, *Oxford Concordance Program: Users' Manual Version 2.0*. Oxford: Oxford University Computing Service, 1988.

Jakobson, Roman, 'Concluding statement: linguistics and poetics', *Style in Language*, ed. T. A. Sebeok. Cambridge, Mass.: MIT Press, 1960.

Johnson Samuel, *Samuel Johnson*, ed. Donald Greene. Oxford and New York: Oxford University Press, 1984.

Keats, John, *The Poems of John Keats*, Annotated English Poets, ed. Miriam Allott. London and New York: Longman and Norton, 1970 and 1972.

Leavis, F. R., *Revaluation: Tradition and Development in English Poetry*. Harmondsworth: Penguin, 1967; first published 1936.

Le Comte, Edward S., '*Areopagitica* as a scenario for *Paradise Lost*', *Achievements of the Left Hand: Essays on the Prose of John Milton*, ed. Michael Lieb and John T. Shawcross. Amherst: University of Massachusetts Press, 1974.

Le Comte, Edward S., *A Dictionary of Puns in Milton's English Poetry*. London and Basingstoke: Macmillan, 1981.

Leishman, J. B. *Milton's Minor Poetry*. London: Hutchinson, 1969.

Lodge, David, 'After Bakhtin', *The Linguistics of Writing: Arguments Between Language and Literature*, ed. Nigel Fabb, Derek Attridge, Alan Durant and Colin MacCabe. London: Macmillan, 1987.

Milic, Louis Tonko, *A Quantitative Approach to the Style of Jonathan Swift*. The Hague: Mouton, 1967.

Miller, Leo, *John Milton and the Oldenburg Safeguard*. New York: Loewenthal, 1985.

Milner, Andrew, *John Milton and the English Revolution*. London and Basingstoke: Macmillan, 1981.

Muller, Charles, 'Lexical distribution reconsidered: the Waring–Herdan formula', *Statistics and Style*, ed. Lubomír Doležel and Richard W. Bailey. New York: American Elsevier.

Ohmann, Richard, 'Generative grammar and the concept of literary style', *Word*, 20 (1964), pp. 423–39.

Ohmann, Richard, 'Literature as sentences', *College English*, 27 (1966), pp. 261–7.

Oras, Ants, 'Milton's early rhyme schemes and the structure of *Lycidas*', *Modern Philology*, 52 (1954), pp. 12–22.

Parker, W.R., letter to *The Times Literary Supplement*, 2 January 1937, p. 12.

Partridge, A. C., *The Language of Renaissance Poetry: Spenser, Shakespeare, Donne, Milton*. London: André Deutsch, 1971.

Raleigh, Sir Walter, *Milton*. London: Edward Arnold, 1900.

Ricks, Christopher, *Milton's Grand Style*. London, Oxford and New York: Oxford University Press, 1967; first published 1963.

Schindler, Walter, *Voice and Crisis: Invocation in Milton's Poetry*. Hamden, Conn.: Archon, 1984.

Sebeok, T. A., ed., *Style in Language* (Cambridge, Mass.: MIT Press, 1960).

Spenser, Edmund, *Poetical Works*, ed. E. De Selincourt. London: Oxford University Press, 1966; first published 1912.

Sprat, Thomas, *History of the Royal Society*, ed. Jackson I. Cope and Harold Whitmore Jones. St Louis, Miss. and London: Washington University Press and Routledge and Kegan Paul, 1966; first published 1959.

SPSS^x User's Guide. New York: McGraw-Hill, 1983.

Stocker, Margarita, *Paradise Lost: An Introduction to the Variety of Criticism*. Basingstoke: Macmillan, 1988.

Sylvester, Joshua, tr. *Divine Weeks and Works of Du Bartas*, ed. Susan Snyder. Oxford: Clarendon Press, 1972.

Thorne, J. P., 'Generative grammar and stylistic analysis', *New Horizons in Linguistics*, ed. John Lyons. Harmondsworth: Penguin, 1970.

Treip, Mindele, *Milton's Punctuation and Changing English Usage 1582–1678*. London: Methuen, 1970.

Vickers, Brian, *Francis Bacon and Renaissance Prose*. Cambridge: Cambridge University Press, 1968.

Waldock, A. J. A., *Paradise Lost and its Critics*. Cambridge: Cambridge University Press, 1947.

Wilding, Michael, *Dragons Teeth: Literature in the English Revolution*. Oxford: Clarendon Press, 1987.

Wit Restor'd. London: 1658.

Index of Passages Cited

The numbers on the left refer to line numbers mentioned in the text; those on the right refer to page numbers in this volume.

Index of Words Discussed

General Index

DATE DUE

FEB 0 5 1998

OCT 2 6 2001

Printed
in USA